THE COURTYARD

A MEMOIR

BENJAMIN PARKET

ALEXA MORRIS

ISBN 9789493418028 (ebook)

ISBN 9789493418004 (paperback)

ISBN 9789493418011 (hardcover)

Publisher: Amsterdam Publishers, The Netherlands, 2025

info@amsterdampublishers.com

The Courtyard is part of the series Holocaust Survivor Memoirs World War II

Copyright © Alexa Morris 2025

Book Cover Design/Illustration: Barış Şehri

CONTENTS

To the countless unrecognized individuals who, at great risk to themselves, came to the aid of Jews during the Holocaust.

וְאָהַבְתָּ לְרֵעֲךָ כָּמוֹךָ.

Love thy neighbor as yourself.
Leviticus 19:18.

1

INVISIBLE

When we hid from the Nazis, we took nothing. Not the handmade quilt from my bed, with its cheerful blue and green squares, though it would have made sleeping on the stone floor those first nights much easier. Not a single dented pot or pan, which would have given us a way to cook, or at least heat some water for tea. Not one book to read. Not the clay marbles that normally were stuffed in my pockets – not even the new agate I won that day from my friend Marcel. I didn't bring the toy wooden boat that I sailed each Sunday at the Jardin du Luxembourg pond with the sail that my mother had patched with a bit of my father's handkerchief. (Oh, how I cried the day that sail ripped. I didn't cry the day we hid because I didn't understand.) Not our radio because, of course, they had taken our radio a long time before that day.

We took the yellow stars because they were attached to the clothes we wore.

"Bring nothing, nothing at all," my father instructed. "It must appear as if we've gone far away – too far to bring any of our belongings."

We were having lunch when Madame Nicolas warned us that the gendarmes were coming. That our names were on a list. Even my name, the name of a French-born nine-year-old boy, was on their list. We were eating meatloaf, mashed potatoes, and beets when she knocked at the door. Once my brothers and I saw the alarm in our parents' eyes, once they started whispering with her in the corner of our small apartment, we stopped eating. We watched and we waited and the meatloaf grew cold while the beets bled purple on our plates.

I say that we took nothing, but I'm sure my mother would have brought some food, probably cheese and bread wrapped in cloth and stuffed into the pockets of her dress. How else would we have eaten those first few days? But other than that, we took nothing at all. We crossed the courtyard in a line, like creeping cartoon mice. And then we went into a hole in the wall and hid from the cat lurking outside, the one who wanted to kill us.

We hid in that single room behind that wall for the next two years. We tried to be invisible so the Nazis would forget about us. We watched the world from our window like ghosts who desperately want to rejoin the living but know they cannot. We were the lucky ones.

2

JULY 1937 – BASTILLE DAY

My earliest memory is of biting into a hot dog, the meaty pop of the first mouthful, and the warm juice running down my chin. I was four years old, standing under the gray Parisian sky at the 1937 World's Fair. The hot dog, presented to me by a smiling American in white shirtsleeves, was the most exotic food in the world.

"What do you think, Binem?" Papa asked. "Is it good, this American sausage?"

"Delicious!" I proclaimed, my mouth full. My older brothers, Sevek and Henri, nodded their agreement, their mouths similarly stuffed.

"Well, where should we go next?" Papa said, unfolding the crisp exhibit guide and squinting at it, a cigarette dangling from his lips.

Where should we go? Everywhere. We traveled the world, right there in Paris. The 1937 Paris Exposition covered 260 acres, with 44 countries participating. The theme – the union of art with the wonders of modern technology – had been conceived in the optimistic 1920s. Opening in the politically charged '30s, the Exposition was plagued by strikes and delays. Still, all of Europe visited – including two of my mother's siblings – her older sister, Baltsza, who had come from Warsaw, and her younger sister Maryla, who visited from Brussels. My mother wore her best flowered dress, her carefully curled hair down and parted on the right, a black handbag resting in the crook of her left arm. My father was a coiled spring in a crisp black suit, trilby hat tilted on his head. Severin, 12 years old, absorbed the sights quietly while Henri, an 11-year-old blond-haired blur, dashed around as if he wanted to see everything at once. It was Bastille Day, July 14, and we stayed until late at night to watch the fireworks light up the sky behind the Eiffel Tower. I sat on my father's shoulders, my brothers in front of us; my mother stood arm-in-arm with her two sisters, the fireworks reflected in their delighted faces.

Many notable French artists had been engaged to develop art for the Exposition. For the Pavilion of Light and Electricity, the Fauvist artist Raoul Dufy painted La Fée Électricité, a 6,500-square-foot fresco. The painting curved around the entire interior of the pavilion, enveloping us in swathes of slowly changing colors.

"This one is about the history of electricity," Severin said, translating the French description for our parents and aunts. My parents, Polish immigrants who unlike their two older children had not had the benefit of going to school in France, spoke only rudimentary French and could not read it. The mural depicted people who contributed to the development of electricity, from Aristotle to Alexander Graham Bell. "Electricity, that *is* quite an invention," said Papa. We had one electric light in our apartment, and it seemed like magic.

In the immense Aeronautics pavilion, we stared at the latest developments in aircraft design and innovation. Inside the echoing hangar were airplanes, planes that were soon to drop explosives all over Europe. Polished, dent-free bombers rested on pedestals under an illuminated ceiling. Visitors ran their hands over the gleaming metal bodies that lay there like sleeping monsters. "Someday, maybe I'll fly a plane like that," Henri said, and he zoomed through the building with his arms extended.

A water taxi took us to a series of manmade islands in the middle of the Seine. From Moroccan markets to the crafts of Indochina, the islands were crowded with temporary constructions representing cities and villages from France's far-flung colonial conquests. Africans stood in grass skirts and wooden tribal masks, stoically shivering in the European summer, so unlike their own. Parisian children lurched by on camels, and swift-fingered Vietnamese created embroidered paintings from the shimmering threads of silkworms.

"Rikla," Aunt Baltsza called out, "Maryla, look at how beautiful this is."

She rubbed a piece of the fine silk fabric between her fingers and waved them over. "It's amazing, I've never seen anything like it." The sisters cooed over the colors and the texture. Raised in the soot and gray stone of Warsaw, they were accustomed to rough woolens and, at best, knobby cotton.

There was no shortage of traditional carnival entertainment either. For a few francs, you could feel the stomach jolt of a roller coaster, be dazzled by the sleight of hand of a mustached magician, or catch a glimpse of a naked woman. The most daring men braved the Avion exhibit where, harnessed into an open parachute, they leapt off a tower and drifted gently to the ground.

"Papa, Papa, will you do that?" we begged. We wanted to watch our brave, strong father jump from the tall metal scaffolding. My mother's eyes widened in horror at the idea.

"No," he said, "because what's going to happen to all of you if my parachute fails?" He smiled and kept walking. "Can't get rid of me that easily," he winked at Mama.

"Oh my," Aunt Baltsza clucked as she stared up. "Why in the world would anyone want to do that?"

"Actually," she admitted, pursing her lips in a gesture that I'd seen my mother do many times, "*my* Sevek might. I'm glad he's not here."

Aunt Baltsza had three children; her oldest, then 18 years old, was named Sevek, which was Severin's Polish name. "Good thing," she added, putting her arm through that of my mother's as they resumed their stroll, "that yours has more sense."

As we wandered back toward the Eiffel Tower, we came to the main attraction of the Exposition: the German and Soviet pavilions. The two exhibits were planted across from each other, separated by the newly built Trocadero Gardens. Germany and Russia, longstanding ideological enemies and competitors, had exhibits that appeared to be confronting each other. The Soviet entry was a sturdy marble edifice that served as a pedestal for a pair of 25-meter-tall figures – a man holding a hammer in his raised arm and a farm woman wielding a sickle in hers – who strode forward from atop the building as though from the prow of a ship. Facing the Soviet pavilion was the German entry, a mausoleum-like structure of rectangular columns topped by a huge bronze eagle, wings extended, talons grasping a swastika. Each building was stark and imposing, designed to impress rather than please, and each cast a long shadow over the crowds. But the German pavilion was a full 20 meters taller, thanks to the fact that Hitler's architect, Albert Speer, had secretly obtained the architectural plans for the Soviet pavilion and designed Germany's so that it would overpower their rival's.

"Why are there so many people here?" Severin asked, peering at the crowds as we stood between the two exhibits, his blue eyes made enormous by thick, black-framed glasses. There were no wild animals, no fire-eaters, no Ferris wheel. What was so exciting?

"Mama, can we go to the roller coaster now?" Henri asked, tugging on my mother's hand.

"In a moment," she replied.

My father wanted to linger. These two pavilions cast a metaphorical shadow alongside the actual one. They were a powerful reminder, amid the largely celebratory pavilions, that very real politics were at play in the larger world. I suspect my father wondered if this faceoff amid the bustling expo portended something more serious than an architectural competition.

Most of the memories of that day have the faded and unmoored quality of a dream, but one event remains sharp in my mind: We lost Henri. One moment he was walking along with us and the next he was gone, swallowed by the crowds. I remember my mother's eyes, the wild look of panic as she spun around, scouring the crowds.

Aunt Baltsza's hand tightened around mine as if I might also slip away, and in an instant the Expo went from exhilarating to terrifying, with the crowds closing in on us, conspiring to block our way. My father, pale and tight-faced, pushed through, sweat blooming under his armpits. My mother's thick, carefully coifed hair quickly became damp, the edges of her curls fraying like a cut cord as she tried to keep up with him. I was yanked along as they searched, their fear a contagion that I felt fluttering within me, too.

It's the fear that remains vivid, the feeling that my parents were not in control, that they were terrified. In 1937, I was still a young boy, and it was the first time I had seen the feral light of fear in their eyes; it would not be the last.

We found Henri at the Expo police station, unharmed but with tear-stained cheeks, a gendarme's kepi on his head. The gendarmes – the French police charged with keeping the public safe – were our protectors, and we trusted them. Their motto, *pro patria vigilans* [watching the country], would soon mean something different, at least for us.

It's ironic that on that Wednesday in 1937, 14 de Juillet, the day that France celebrates its liberation and independence, a day known as Bastille Day after the destruction of a prison that symbolized injustice and despotism, new prisons were already being built around us, though we could not see them yet. By the time the gendarmes knocked on our door in 1941, Aunt Baltsza was already confined behind the walls of the Warsaw Ghetto. How could we know that when we said goodbye to her after her visit, when we hugged her at the Gare du Nord before she boarded her train, we were saying goodbye forever? That when she bent and smiled at us through the train window, waving as it pulled away, that it would be the last time we saw her face?

Standing on the platform of the Eiffel Tower and looking at the crowds below celebrating the French Republic and all that it stood for, how could we possibly imagine that my father would soon be behind the barbed wire of the Nazi-run camp, Drancy? That in five years – almost to the day – our family would quietly slip into a dusty workshop to hide from the same police who protected Henri that day.

But on that beautiful July day, as we wandered the exposition grounds and gaped at the glistening buildings and the people who looked like no one we'd ever seen before, it seemed as if the future was a bright and shiny thing.

July 1937, before heading to the International Exposition of Art and Technology in Modern Life in Paris. Left to right, back row: Rikla, Joseph, Baltsza, Maryla. Front row: Henri, me, Severin.

3

1931 – A NEW LIFE

My father smelled of varnish the way other fathers smell of cologne, sweat, or whiskey: It came from his pores, as though from somewhere deep inside. Even now, when I inhale the sharp, wintery scent of lacquer, I think of him.

He was a *vernisseur* [varnisher], a trade he'd learned in Warsaw. He moved to Paris in 1931 at the suggestion of his sister, my Aunt Sabine – previously known as Shayndl – who had immigrated to Paris from Poland in the 1920s. Aunt Sabine and her husband, Israel, had an apartment near the Place de la République, where her nimble fingers sewed party dresses for the wealthy in the sun-filled atelier attached to their apartment. She wrote to my father, told him how happy she was, and suggested he join them there.

He didn't need much encouragement. My father felt France offered great promise – it beckoned to him, a propitious dream – at a time when Poland was in a bad way. The Depression hit Poland in 1930, well before it hit Western Europe. Unemployment was at 20 percent; the price of crops dropped dramatically and barrels of grain sat unsold and fermenting in warehouses, feeding only rats. In Warsaw, men with pleading eyes and stained suits lined the streets, clinking tin cups to beg for food and spare change. Though my father was a skilled varnisher, there was little opportunity to grow a business. He knew that to build a life for his family, he needed to leave Poland.

When he arrived in Paris, he found his way to the 11th arrondissement, a neighborhood known for woodworking. After walking the streets and looking at ateliers to lease, he eventually spotted the arched stone tunnel that leads into 5 rue de Charonne. Rue de Charonne cuts diagonally through the lower half of the IIth arrondissement, curving like an upside-down spoon, with 5 rue de Charonne at the westward tip of the spoon, the entry gate just steps before the street intersects the main artery of rue du Faubourg Saint-Antoine. It isn't a single building but four, forming a rectangle five floors high and surrounding a large courtyard. In the 1930s, most units were ateliers filled with tradesmen – carpenters, varnishers, and upholsters – some of whom, like my father, also had apartments facing the same courtyard. I imagine that as he saw the courtyard bustling with workers like himself, he knew he'd found a home. He was greeted by the concierge, Madame Raymond, an imposing Frenchwoman who always had a ring of skeleton keys in her hand or stuffed into one of her pockets. I don't know if she immediately sized him up as a good man or if he right away recognized the kindness behind her stern demeanor, but they would eventually become good friends. He signed a contract and went to work building his business. A year later, my mother and two brothers – I hadn't been born yet – joined him.

Did my mother also want to emigrate? She was 34 years old with two exuberant young sons. The family was living in cramped quarters, sharing a dim single-room apartment in a coal-streaked building with her mother. Several of her siblings had already fled Poland seeking brighter futures: Aunt Maryla and a brother were in Belgium, another sister was in Argentina. So the idea of leaving Warsaw must have seemed plausible, and shortly it was agreed upon. My father would go ahead to Paris, find housing and employment, and send for his family once settled.

In the summer of 1931, while the shifting faces of dark clouds threatened rain, my mother and brothers went to the Chmielna Street Railway Station to see my father off. I've imagined the scene many times. It must have been hard for my father to leave his family, and I can picture him, squatting in front of seven-year-old Sevek and six-year-old Henek – my brothers' names before their Polish names were changed to French– and putting his hands on their shoulders. "I will send for you as soon as I can, but you are both growing so quickly that I'm sure you will be much taller when I see you next," he said. "In the meantime, take care of your mother for me." He hugged them both and, picking up his suitcase, stepped onto the train. My mother watched until the train became a pinprick on the horizon.

I'm sure there were other wives on the platform that day watching their husbands leave – wives who, like my mother, were consigned to wait hopefully and anxiously for a letter saying it was time to follow, time to leave everyone you know, time to head out for a new country, a new language, a new life. And while they waited for their letter – sometimes months, sometimes years – they worried. What if it was hard for him to find work?

What if he met another woman, a sophisticated Parisian with full red lips that whispered promises of a different, better life? Or, what if when she arrived at her new home, she could not adjust? What if she became lonely and missed her family in Poland?

One year later, the postman pulled the longed-for letter from his mailbag and handed it to her. In the summer of 1932, Mama, Sevek, and Henek packed up the few belongings they could take with them and, waving goodbye to Grandma Baele, boarded a train to Paris. My mother may have been nervous, but to my brothers it seemed the steam engine let out a jubilant shout, the whoop of adventure, as they left. My father met them at the Gare du Nord in a pinstriped suit, his hair smoothed back, his right toe tapping in anticipation. He marveled at how the boys had grown, took my mother's suitcase with a peck on her cheek, and brought them to their new home.

The small apartment at 5 rue de Charonne was clean and tidy and in the center, on a wooden table, my father had placed something my mother and brothers had never seen before – a bowl of oranges. They were the promise of a sweet, bright future.

Sevek, inspecting an orange, turned it in his hand. He held it to his nose and inhaled the lush, heady scent. Can you think of another fruit whose scent fills the air like an orange does? French royalty famously grew oranges just to make perfume from their blossoms: Louis XIV had the fragrance made from his trees at Versailles. Marie Antoinette used to dabble orange blossom perfume on her neck, and even revolutionaries such as Napoleon wore the scent.

"Here, let me show you," my father said.

The orange, like a present, must be unwrapped to be enjoyed. With each tug of the peel, the fruit mists the air until, naked, the orange reveals itself to be made for sharing.

Papa held out the peeled orange and my brothers devoured the fruit, licking the juice from their sticky fingers. My mother laughed, "Your father will think I've been starving you both."

My brothers entered school at the École Keller, a short walk away. One of the first major changes they experienced was their names. Until then they'd been known by their Polish names, but French schools required French appellations, so Sevek became Severin and Henek became Henri. They adapted to their new country as easily as to their new names, quickly learning the French language and the French way of life. They made new friends, playing marbles in the school courtyard instead of *serso* [hoop & stick game] on the streets of Warsaw.

When I was a young boy not yet old enough to go to school, I liked nothing more than watching the courtyard's artisans, especially my father, at work. The courtyard was a hive of activity, tradesmen buzzing in and out of the stairways, or doorways, and I loved being in the center of it, amazed by the industry whirling around me. And if the courtyard was a hive, the queen bee was our concierge. Known affectionately as *La Pipelette* [The Concierge], Madame Raymond was the unofficial matron of 5 rue de Charonne. Built like an armoire with dark, caterpillar brows, she lived on the ground floor of Stairway 1 with her husband and two grown children, René and Paulette.

There were 13 stairways to the various ateliers. They ran counterclockwise around the courtyard, with Stairway 1 at the northeast corner. We lived on the second floor of Stairway 1, two flights up a spiral staircase. While other stairways mostly led to commercial ateliers, Stairway 1 was the notable exception, with most of its units being apartments.

Each afternoon, my mother made Papa a snack, and I crossed the courtyard from our apartment to his atelier in Stairway 9 to deliver his paper-wrapped sandwich and thermos of tea. "Let's see what we have today," he would say with a seemingly genuine curiosity, though it was almost always meatloaf. As he unfolded the paper and dug in, I sat down on the floor, crossed my legs, and tucked into my own, smaller sandwich.

On occasion, the afternoon snack was a sandwich of kielbasa or some other cured meat, Mama would have procured it from the Meyers' charcuterie. The Meyers were a middle-aged couple who lived across the hall from the Raymonds on the ground floor of Stairway 1. They owned the charcuterie that faced rue de Charonne, which was also accessible from a back door within the courtyard. The shop window was partially filled with dangling ham hocks and chains of curing salami and the store smelled of smoked meat and sauerkraut. Monsieur Meyer spent his days stuffing sausages, his stomach bulging behind his white apron. His grown daughter, who had a serious stutter that made her shy and wary of conversation, worked the register, her eyes always cast down.

The thermos I carried to my father contained hot tea, made from tea leaves that came in a metal tin from the *épicerie* [grocery store] next door to the Meyers' charcuterie. Not one to waste anything, Mama always held on to the tea tins after they were empty and used them to store other items. I had one, too, which I used for my clay marbles. The épicerie was owned by the Reginauds, who lived directly above the Meyers on the first floor – the first floor in France being what we in America call the second floor – of Stairway

1. The Reginauds were older than my parents, with soft pillowy bodies and matching gray hair that curled like steel wool.

I didn't know it then, but these three families – the Raymonds, the Meyers, and the Reginauds – would play a pivotal role in my life.

A varnisher's work is very physical. My father stood all day, bending over furniture and putting the force of his body into his movements. Deliveries of antique furniture arrived at the cobblestone courtyard in horse-drawn carriages. The furniture was carried up the narrow spiral stairs to his workshop by huffing men, the briny odor of their sweat lingering long after they'd clattered back downstairs. Commodes, armoires, chairs with cartouche-shaped backs and cabriole legs: They all arrived bruised and scuffed. By the time he was done with each piece it was restored and lustrous, but the effort took a toll on his body, and each night he came home drained. His strong and ropey arms were spent; they hung at his side, limp and heavy.

When he was in the right mood, he told me stories while he worked. Stories of how he'd met my mother, of how different life was back in Poland. Some of my favorites were about his time as a soldier in the Polish-Soviet War. I burned with the typical boyhood romanticization of military battle and, while he indulged my fascination, he also made sure to share the less pleasant aspects such as episodes of antisemitism he'd faced from many of the Christian soldiers.

"Some were fine with Jews, of course, but others gave me a hard time," he said. He paused to blow the sawdust from the table he was sanding and leaned in close, squinting and moving his left index finger over the scratch to determine whether he'd smoothed it sufficiently. His left index finger was the only index finger he had: His right one ended at the knuckle, a casualty of a hammer accident long before I was born. I loved to hold on to the stub when we walked together. "Once I was confronted in the mess hall," he continued. "I was walking with my tray, looking for a place to sit when another soldier told me I needed to take off my cap." He pointed to his head. "It was a military issue cap, not a *béret*."

For the largely Christian military population, removing a hat when indoors was a customary and respectful tradition. However, it is not a Jewish tradition, and my father felt no obligation to adhere to it.

"After all, on Yom Kippur, when we enter the synagogue, we put *on* our *kippahs*, correct?" Papa asked. I nodded. This was true. While we were not religious, we dutifully attended synagogue on the major holidays and, when we did, we wore our kippahs.

"Of course, I was not wearing a kippah, I was wearing my soldier's cap. But it doesn't matter: A Jew doesn't need to remove his hat when he's indoors. A Christian may have this obligation, but we are not Christian. So I said, 'No, I don't need to take it off.' And I started to walk away. But he yelled after me, again, 'You must remove your cap when you are indoors.'"

"What did you do?"

"Well, at this point some other soldiers had started to notice. They'd stopped their own conversations and were paying attention to us. So first I put down my tray." Father, his hands dusted with fine wood fibers, mimicked the setting down of a mess hall tray, very slowly and deliberately. "And then I convinced him that he was wrong." Papa held his fists up like a boxer.

"It turned out that, in the end, he saw it my way," Father said with a smile. "So I found a seat, and I ate my dinner."

When my father was not in the mood for stories, or when he was very busy, he sent me away. On those days I would wander across the hallway to visit Monsieur Sherapan, a much older man who made furniture in an adjacent workshop. I liked to watch him work, and he always welcomed me into his atelier. His ancient body was bent from years of hard labor and his back curled like a gnarled question mark over his workbench.

"You are very old Monsieur Sherapan," I frequently observed, with the guileless honesty of the very young. "Why are you still working?"

"I'm fond of eating, my boy," he would always answer. "And if I do not work, I cannot eat."

And so work he did. His hands, twisted like tree branches, moved slowly but steadily, holding years of accumulated skill in their arthritic grip.

Still, my favorite person to watch, my favorite person in the world, was my father. When he called across the courtyard for his afternoon snack, I delighted in delivering it. On rare occasions, his ulcer flared up and he came home before noon and didn't return to work. He lay down with a warm compress on his stomach, eyes closed and lips tight with pain. The doctor recommended filet mignon to coat his stomach, so Mama and I took the Métro to a butcher in Belleville and came home with the steak wrapped in a tidy paper package. I watched as she grilled it over the stove, flames licking the basket.

While he ate, I stood next to him, tapping my fingers on the table until he asked, "Is this your meal, Goldener Kop, or is it mine?" Goldener Kop, Yiddish for "golden head," was his term of endearment, and when he used it, I knew I would get my way.

"It's *our* dinner, Tatush," I said.

Smiling, he raised his fork to me and the steak melted in my eager mouth.

Of the three children in my family, I was the only one born in France. My mother later told me how much she loved being pregnant in Paris; she was delighted to find that our courtyard neighbors were as excited and protective of her growing belly as she was. Our upstairs neighbor, Madame Nicolas, insisted on carrying any bags up the stairs for my pregnant mother. A young widow with a heart-shaped, porcelain doll face and ocean-blue eyes, Madame Nicolas worked at the central police station, where she typed up memos for officers. "*Madame, vous devez prendre soin de toi et du bébé* [You must take care of yourself, and your baby]!" she would say when she spied my mother, waddling with her bags in her hands, returning from the market. And she would take the bags from her and charge up the stairs. Little could my mother have known that, less than ten years later, Madame Nicolas would risk everything to save our lives.

A healthy, squalling baby, I came into the world on Monday, August 28, 1933, at the Hôpital Saint-Antoine on the rue du Faubourg Saint-Antoine. From my mother I received blue eyes, a fair complexion, a quick smile, and hair the color of corn silk; from my father, a striving, restless ambition. Born eight years after Henri, I would always be the baby, the favorite; I was destined to be indulged.

"Hello, Binem," my father whispered, holding my closed fist as he gazed at me. "Hello, my little Frenchman."

I was named after a distant relative, and my birth record shows that my name was recorded as Binem Parket, rather than my family name of Parkiet. Some quick-moving and distracted nurse, perhaps interrupted as she was scrawling down my name, omitted the "i." To my brothers and my friends in Paris, I would be Bernard. To my parents, I was always Binem.

In January of that year, Adolf Hitler became chancellor of Germany, and by the time of my birth, he'd managed to dissolve all the other political parties; the Nazi Party was the only party that remained. Once he ascended to power, *Mein Kampf*, the rambling autobiographical treatise he'd dictated to cellmates in 1925 while in prison after attempting a coup d'état, became a bestseller. Describing his path to antisemitism and his hatred of Communism – Jews and communists were the twin evils of his time, as he saw it – *Mein Kampf* was given to each newly married German couple on their wedding day, a gift from the state. Congratulations on your marriage, and Heil Hitler. The longstanding antisemitism that had simmered for years in Germany was starting to erupt in small, poisonous bubbles. On April 1, Hitler ordered a nationwide boycott of Jewish-owned businesses, and steel-faced stormtroopers blocked access to shops that had been painted with a yellow-and-black Star of David. Though the official boycott lasted for only one day, it was the flint that sparked the many informal boycotts to follow.

At the time, in France, these happenings were nothing more than a rumor, a whisper, the pale sound of distant thunder on a sunny day. This was soon to change.

First photograph of me as a baby.

4

SPRING 1938 – BROKEN GLASS

My best friend was a girl named Renée, but we called her Titi. I was three, maybe four when we first met. It's hard to be certain because I don't remember a time before her. We shared a love of hide-and-seek and *pain au chocolat*. What didn't we have in common? Well, she had brown bouncing curls while I had straight blond hair. She was a girl, and I was a boy. I was Jewish. She was not. These differences caused us the same level of concern, which is to say, none whatsoever.

Titi lived with her parents in an apartment off Stairway 3. There weren't any other young children in our courtyard and, while we were initially thrust together by proximity and age, it turned out we were natural playmates, and she became my first and best childhood friend. In those days boys and girls were educated separately in France, but our schools, like our homes, were adjacent to each other. Titi and I walked to grammar school together, parting at the entrance of École Keller as I went left into *l'école de garçons* [the boys' school] and she went into *l'école de filles* [the girls' school] on the right. We met up again in the afternoon to walk home, often stopping on the way to get a pain au chocolat from Madame Benot's boulangerie.

On rainy winter afternoons we ran, scooting between the black umbrellas of other pedestrians and splashing in puddles along the way. Once in our courtyard, I would race up Stairway 1 with Titi behind me; the wooden soles of my galoshes slapped the stairs as I leapt up, two steps at a time, and the wood-on-wood sound reverberated loudly throughout the spiral staircase. Thwack! Thwack! THWACK! THWACK! It drove our neighbor Madame Poirier crazy. She and her husband lived directly across the second-floor landing from our apartment. They had no children and seemed less than delighted to be living across from our lively family. "Bernard!" she shouted, leaning out her door and looking down the spiral as I launched myself up. "Ber-NARD!" She yelled again, her face pinched and angry beneath a crown of tightly bound gray hair. Titi and I slowed, walking with great restraint until we came to my door. Then, forgetting my manners, I pushed the door open enthusiastically and it slammed against the inside wall, startling my mother, who was standing over a pot on the cast iron stove. I threw my bag, galoshes, and coat on the floor in a puddle, then pulled off my school smock.

"Binem, must you really make such a dramatic entrance?" My mother looked me over. "And such a wet one?" She shook her head indulgently.

"Yes, Mama, I must." I said it almost apologetically, as if I were genuinely sorry that the situation called for me to be so theatrical, but that I was reluctantly compelled to do it. Some things are just unavoidable.

My family lived in a two-room apartment. It was originally one room, a large rectangle, but when we moved in, Papa divided it by building a hollow plywood wall down the middle. He covered the wall in flowery paper, intricate red roses encircled by wreaths of laurel leaves on a pale blue background. My parents' bed was in the street-side half, with floor-to-ceiling casement windows facing rue de Charonne. My brothers and I shared the other side of the apartment with a well-worn dining table and the stove, which sat in the corner, creaking and sighing like an elderly family member who does not want to be forgotten. Our single window faced the interior courtyard. My bed was a metal rollaway that we unfolded each night, and my brothers slept against the opposite wall, where Henri had a trundle that pulled out from under Severin's bed. There was a tiny sink next to our stove, but on the stone landing outside our front door was a larger porcelain sink, chipped and ribboned with rust, that we shared with our neighbors. The communal toilet was accessed by a door in the wall between the second and third floors off the spiral staircase.

After a quick kiss from my mother, who went back to stir the burbling saucepan, Titi and I dove under my parents' bed, where we liked to play amid the tumbleweeds of dust that collected there despite my mother's near-constant sweeping. In such a small apartment, it was one of the only places we could play out of sight, and we claimed it as our private fort. Now, having slid under the bed, she rolled over on her back. Her curls were wet and flattened against her head, and beads of rainwater freckled her face.

"She's scary," Titi said, meaning Madame Poirier.

I nodded my agreement and said, "Like a witch." Titi pulled a paper bag out of her smock pocket and opened it with a rustle, extracting a flattened chocolate croissant. The melted chocolate squished out of the end like a tongue sticking out at me. I rolled over, too, and faced the underside of my parents' bed. A gray spider with delicate, thread-like legs crept between two wooden boards on the bed frame. Titi ripped the croissant in two and passed half to me, and we lay there on our backs, our eyes fully adjusted to the dim light; the only sound was the smacking of our lips as we devoured the croissant. I watched as the spider completed its peculiar mincing ballet, reaching the end of the boards and disappearing with a bow into the narrow space between the mattress and the frame.

"Did you get in trouble for the window?" Titi asked.

"No, not really."

I was still surprised that I hadn't been punished. A couple of days before, during a break in what had been a stretch of rainy days, kids from the neighborhood had gathered to play football in our courtyard. The courtyard provided a large safe space to play, but its surface was ill-suited for football – the ball bounced unpredictably off the irregular cobblestones, adding a strong dose of luck to a normally skill-based game. That day my own wobbly kick sent the ball spinning sideways in a low arc directly into the ground-floor shop window of Monsieur Herbin's carpentry shop at Stairway 2. Monsieur Herbin made high-end reproductions of classic French furniture for wealthy Parisians: His handcrafted dining tables hosted lavish dinner parties and his cabinets held the fine porcelain and expensive liquor of minor French nobility. He was a fairly high-strung man on the best of days.

We heard the high tinkling sound of breaking glass as the ball went through his window. Everyone froze. The world was silent for one heavy beat, and then Monsieur Herbin burst from his shop with a yell. His face and bald head were tomato red and he brandished a chisel in his hand like a weapon.

At the sight of the furious carpenter all the other kids disappeared, scattering like exposed insects under an overturned log. Only Titi stayed planted where she was, her brown eyes wide and worried.

"Who did this?" Monsieur Herbin pointed to what was left of his window, the chisel waving wildly in his hand. "Someone is going to pay for this!" He looked back and forth between me and Titi.

It was clear that one of us was responsible.

"It was me, Monsieur Herbin," I said. "I'm very sorry. It was an accident." My voice sounded small and thin like it was coming from far away, the words diluted by the distance they had traveled. I didn't want to admit it was me, but it wasn't like I could get out of it. Everyone in the courtyard had seen me kick the ball through his window.

Monsieur Herbin made a visible effort to rein in his temper. "Okay,

Bernard, I'll talk to your father. No more playing ball here today." While this meant I could go, it was hardly a relief. With that, Titi and I silently agreed to part. I slunk back to my apartment to await my punishment, past the sympathetic smile of our concierge's son René who, while sweeping out front of Stairway I, had witnessed everything.

That evening, my father sat me down at the dining table.

"I understand you broke Monsieur Herbin's shop window today," Papa said. "Something about playing ball in the courtyard." He pulled a pack of Gauloise cigarettes from his front shirt pocket, tamping it on the table. "He came to talk to me. He was upset." That was an understatement: I'd seen veins running rivers across Monsieur Herbin's bald crown and spittle exploding from his mouth.

I nodded, mute. Rather than look at my father, I stared at the table, at the water marks left by the countless glasses that had rested on it. Slouched down in my chair, I traced the waxy half-moons with my finger as if it were important work needing my utmost attention.

Henri, sitting at the other end of the table, looked up from a model ship he was building and laughed. He was forever building models. My parents had learned that his hands caused less trouble if occupied.

"What happened Bernard, did you lose your temper and throw something at him?" Henri joked.

"No!" I turned and glared at my brother.

My father, frowning slightly, ignored him.

When I was four years old, I accidentally shattered the mirrored face of my parents' wardrobe. I was playing with wooden blocks on the floor and Henri, in the way that only siblings can, teased me until I lost my temper and threw a block at him. I missed, hitting the mirror instead. A long crack appeared, spreading out like a spider web. My father had been furious with me at the time, and the mirror was cracked to this day.

Papa, an unlit cigarette wedged in the corner of his mouth, seemed deep in thought as he scraped a tiny bit of varnish off his thumb. "Binem, I'm not angry," he said. "I know that you didn't do it intentionally, and I know that you feel bad about it. Accidents happen. You know I do a lot of work for Monsieur Herbin, and we will figure this out."

Monsieur Herbin was one of my father's longstanding clients. Papa took the Louis XV reproductions that Monsieur Herbin crafted and buffed the virgin wood until the pieces could pass for originals.

"I hope it was a good kick at least," he added. I smiled back at him now, a weight lifted.

"Did you know, Binem," he asked, leaning back in his chair, "that broken glass has a special meaning in Judaism?"

My father's only education had been a religious one. He spent his youth *davening* [praying] in the *shul* [synagogue], studying only the Torah. While he'd long ago shrugged off the restrictive bindings of orthodoxy, he still retained a good amount of accumulated religious knowledge.

"You mean like in a wedding?" I asked. By then I knew it was a Jewish tradition to break a wine glass under your foot when you got married. The groom stomps on the glass as the couple stands under the *chuppah* [ritual canopy]. With the breaking of the glass, the couple is officially married.

My father nodded. "But it goes back farther than that," he said. "There is a reason why that tradition exists. We break a glass to remind us of a time when things were harder, when we were enslaved by the Romans many, many years ago. Our people were sick of being slaves and we rebelled against the Romans, but they were much more powerful than us. They came to Jerusalem and they ransacked our city. They destroyed the Holy Temple. Hundreds of Jews were slaughtered and the rebellion was crushed, and thousands were enslaved once again."

"What does that have to do with a broken glass?" I asked. "And why would people want to remember that when they are getting married? Was there someone getting married in the Holy Temple when the Romans arrived?" None of this made sense.

My father smiled. "Those are good questions, Binem. Tell me, if I crush a glass with my foot, can you put it back together?"

I shook my head. You only had to take a look at the remainder of Monsieur Herbin's window, at the tiny pieces that covered the ground like diamonds, to know it would be impossible to put back together.

"Right. If someone brings me a broken piece of furniture, I can almost always fix it. Wood is forgiving that way. But when you break something made of glass, it's permanent.

"And so is marriage," he said, nodding in Mama's direction. "So the breaking of the glass symbolizes the irrevocable covenant that the couple has made in joining themselves together." Mama looked up from her knitting and smiled at both of us.

"There are other interpretations, too," he continued. "Some people say that it's a reminder that there is sadness even in the most joyous of moments. Such is the history of our people. There has been much sadness in our journey.

"Anyway," he finished, "it's just a window. It's replaceable."

Within a week, a new window arrived, the glass brought by carriage while Monsieur Herbin watched, arms crossed over his chest. I stood with my father as the men gently placed the window into the casing. I saw my serious expression reflected back at me, next to the more whimsical one of my father. Monsieur Herbin, after leaning in to inspect a smudge and wiping it clear with his sleeve, was satisfied.

My father was not yet satisfied. For months after the incident, upon completing a project for Monsieur Herbin, Papa would wink at me as he prepared his invoice and say, "Now I add my special window tax."

My father was right, of course. One broken window isn't a big deal. An entire country of broken windows, a nation of glass shattered by violence and malice, that is another matter entirely. We didn't know it yet, but that winter, the winter of 1938, Jews in Germany would be faced with the destruction of more temples and more stores, and the broken glass would cover the streets in a jagged, glittery dust. Kristallnacht – the Night of Broken Glass – was a harbinger of the violence to come.

Titi (left) and me (right), dressed in costume for a kindergarten play.

5

WINTER 1938 – PREMONITIONS

Aunt Sabine and Uncle Israel liked to entertain, and we went to their apartment often. They lived in a spacious apartment on rue de Crussol, steps from the Oberkampf Métro station. I suppose my aunt enjoyed the socializing, the sound of so much Yiddish being spoken at once – all these friends from Poland laughing together as raucous as a flock of starlings. But I also suspect that she would have preferred the mingling to take place without anyone touching anything. Their home had the staid and formal air of a museum, everything polished and in its place, and my aunt served as its solicitous but stiff docent: friendly, eager for everyone to have a good time, but always monitoring that nothing was damaged or broken. Maybe that's because my uncle tended to move through the apartment – and the world in general – with utter disregard for his surroundings, a smile on his face and a drink in his hand, waving the glass in greeting, its contents splashing over the sides of the tumbler, a maraschino cherry bobbing like a ship in a stormy sea. His warm, handsome face was as open as Aunt Sabine's was closed, and he tousled my hair each time I passed by him.

Aunt Sabine's parquet floors – and she referred to them as *her* floors – were as shiny as glass, and she acted as if they were as fragile. Any scuff left by my leather shoes drew a disappointed frown, and the result was that I traversed them on tiptoes, attempting to move through the apartment as silently and unnoticed as a thief. It was so different from my father's unfussy attitude. Had it not been for the shape of their faces – they shared the same heavy-lidded eyes and the same teardrop of an earlobe – I would not have believed they were related. My father was meticulous about his appearance:

He started each day by putting a razor to his face, and his clothes were always pressed. But the furniture in our home was utilitarian and bore the scars of family life. Perhaps it was because he spent all day repairing nicks and scratches in other people's furniture and knew– better than his sister, certainly – how easily such things could be repaired. Or perhaps it was because he understood the impermanence of polish and how quickly it would fade.

One November evening at Aunt Sabine's, as we gathered over boiled cabbage and brisket, I noticed less laughing and teasing. The conversations took on a tense, urgent tone. Cold air slipped in through the slightly open window and the gas lamps flickered, almost as if the lamps themselves were nervous. Aunt Sabine poured tea and passed it around. The room echoed with the clinking sound of cups being set down on saucers. I listened while the adults talked, eavesdropping while appearing to be paying no attention at all, lest I be sent from the room. My cousins Micheline and Huguette were setting up a doll's tea party in their bedroom, and I had no interest in doing that. Kneeling on my aunt's art deco rug, my metal toy car in hand, I traced the red swooping curves and the sharp gray angles on the wool pile – I pretended they were the twists and turns of a winding road my car took at great speed – and my lips sputtered quietly in imitation of the sound of a motor being revved up.

The adults were discussing Kristallnacht. The word is a combination of *Kristallglas*, which means crystal glass, and *Nacht*, or night. Kristallnacht started on November 9, 1938, and is often considered the beginning of the Holocaust. Working together, Nazi civilians and soldiers smashed the windows of Jewish-owned stores and synagogues in towns and cities throughout Germany and Austria in a rampage that lasted 24 hours. The police were instructed not to intervene. Buildings burned and the streets were covered in broken glass, which is where Kristallnacht got its name. Almost 100 Jewish men were killed, and thousands more were arrested and transferred to labor camps.

Although Kristallnacht took place in Germany, it owed its origin to an event in my home city of Paris. On November 7, 1938, a distraught 17-year-old German-Jewish immigrant named Herschel Grynszpan hastened down rue Marbeau, a small street nestled between two spokes off the Arc du Triomphe. He burst into the German embassy, where he shot a Nazi diplomat named Ernst vom Rath. Grynszpan did not resist arrest, and as he was whisked off to prison he declared that his actions were in protest of "Polenaktion," a recent event in which more than 12,000 Polish-born Jews were expelled from Germany on Hitler's orders. Grynszpan's parents, then living in Hanover, Germany, were among those sent back to Poland with no warning; like all foreigners who were expelled, they were allowed only one suitcase per person to carry all of their worldly belongings.

"Poland already hates its Jews, and Hitler hates the Poles. What will happen to our families now?" my mother asked, directing her question to no one in particular as she cradled her tea between cupped hands. Everyone in the room had family back in Poland. I glanced up from the carpet and saw the adults staring into their teacups as if the answer could be found in the swirling dregs.

It's not known for sure why vom Rath, a mid-level Nazi with no direct involvement in the Polenaktion, was Grynszpan's target. It may be that he just happened to be the first diplomat that Grynszpan encountered when he stormed into the embassy. Whatever his motivations, Grynszpan's actions provided Joseph Goebbels, Hitler's chief of propaganda, the excuse he needed to act against the Jews. Violence broke out all over the Reich, stoked by Nazi leaders who made it clear that they would not interfere. Kristallnacht was presented by the Nazi regime as a spontaneous public outburst provoked by outrage at the assassination, but it was anything but. Kristallnacht was a nationwide, state-sponsored pogrom conducted throughout Germany and Austria. It was calculated and orchestrated by Goebbels and Reinhard Heydrich, Hitler's chief of security.

"I've heard it's much worse in Warsaw now," said a woman with a dry, raspy voice and a face taut with fear. "My cousin tried to come home and was sent away again. There is even talk that Poland will throw out its own Jews, like Germany." I looked up again, waiting to hear what would come next, though I had little sense that any of this would ever affect me.

Throughout the preceding several years, antisemitism had increased in Poland, so much so that in 1937 the Polish government explored the possibility of deporting all of its Jews to the French colony of Madagascar, a remote, humid island near southeastern Africa. The plan was ultimately rejected by Poland due to the island's small size (and by a French government that did not want to be overrun by Polish Jews), but it was to be briefly resuscitated by the Nazis, who thought it might be a way to get rid of their own Jews, before being discarded in favor of the Final Solution.

Things in Germany had gotten dramatically worse throughout 1937 and 1938. By the summer 1938, Jews in Germany had been deprived of almost all rights and property and were emigrating in droves, looking for a better life. The flood of Jewish refugees leaving Nazi Germany presented a challenge – the so-called "Jewish Problem" – for the countries they tried to enter. The issue was severe enough that, in July 1938, US President Franklin Delano Roosevelt called for an international conference in Evian, France, to discuss the fate of the refugees. Germany did not attend, but Hitler, a heckler from the sidelines, offered to deliver Germany's Jews "on luxury ships" to any welcoming nation. While 32 countries participated in the Evian Conference, few of them were willing to accept more immigrants. Hitler mocked the failure of the conference, noting the irony of the very countries criticizing Germany for its treatment of Jews being unwilling to accept them. In the end, the only message the Evian Conference sent – indirectly but clearly by its failure to reach any kind of agreement to help the refugees – was that foreign governments didn't care and would not interfere in Hitler's antisemitic policies. This was a message that Hitler surely heard.

Germany wasn't the only country enacting antisemitic legislation. In January 1938, Romania stripped its Jews of citizenship and then in May 1938, Hungary barred Jews from many professions. But the violence of Kristallnacht marked something new.

Uncle Israel leaned forward in his club chair, his eyes dark. I wasn't accustomed to seeing my gregarious, fun-loving uncle look so serious, and I paused my toy car to watch him. "It is too late for them to come here, though," he said. "It's impossible to get approved." He waved his cigarette in frustration, the smoke swirling, scribbling nonsense. At this point, the French government had effectively frozen all immigration.

"It's too late for anyone to go anywhere," Aunt Sabine said, an unfamiliar hint of dolor in her voice as she bent to sweep crumbs from a side table. "Where can they go?"

It was a good question.

6

FALL OF 1939 – BLITZKRIEG

If you were to look at a map of Europe in 1939, you would see a Germany that surrounded much of Poland's western half, enveloping it to the north and south, like an alligator with open jaws. As Poland waited, vulnerable, a morsel ready to be consumed, its leaders tried to secure protection. In March, Poland signed a treaty with the United Kingdom and France that pledged each nation would support the others if one was invaded. The treaty gave Germany pause; the alligator hesitated, stopping to calculate when and where it should clamp down on the country in its jaws.

Finally, on September 1, it bit. Germany's invasion of Poland is known as the Blitzkrieg, or "lightning war." Reluctantly, out of obligation to fulfill the terms of the Anglo-Polish Agreement, Great Britain and France entered World War II on September 3. Less than a month later, Poland surrendered and the hammer of German boots descended on Warsaw.

After the Blitzkrieg, all Parisians were required to cover their windows so German warplanes couldn't see the glow of our lights at night. Papa brought home the remnants of boxes, and each evening before dusk we applied large swaths of cardboard to our floor-to-ceiling windows, sealing our apartment off from the rest of the world. The light from the setting sun, which normally filled our apartment at dusk, was blotted out.

Paris, the famous City of Lights, had been darkened. All the gas lamps were temporarily extinguished in order to make the city a harder target for the roaming German bombers. Since motorists were prohibited from using headlights, gendarmes wore white capes as they walked the streets at night to make themselves more visible; our city was protected by patrolling ghosts.

Broad white bands were painted at pedestrian crosswalks on the busier Parisian intersections so people knew where it was safe to cross.

While these new happenings were initially exciting to my six-year-old self, nothing fundamental had changed for us. In much of Western Europe, this new war was known as the Phony War; the British press even dubbed it *Sitzkrieg* ["sitting" war] because of the inaction of the Allies during the first eight months. In France, it was known as the *drôle de guerre*, or the "funny" or "strange" war. While we were technically at war, no major military action had taken place.

After dinner, we still played cards around our old table as we had every night since I was old enough to hold them in my hands. We played *belote*, the most popular card game in France, and Papa and I were a team against Henri and Severin. Our father told us stories as we played, often about his time as a soldier in the Polish-Soviet War. Drafted in 1919, he fought for Poland until, during the retreat from the Russian front back toward Warsaw in 1920, he contracted typhus and was discharged. While he was initially proud to fight for his country and defend the socialist causes he believed in, the hostility he encountered from his fellow soldiers left him disillusioned with Poland. On this night, he told us a story we'd never heard before.

"I was in the middle of packing crates, assembling our supplies," he said. "We were getting ready to march to the Russian front. I heard someone behind me, another soldier. He said, 'When we get to the front, *Żyd* [Jew], my first bullet is for you.'"

"He really said that? To you?" Henri asked, disbelieving.

"Yes. And when I turned around, he stared me right in the eye. To make sure I knew he meant it, I guess. Then he just walked away." Papa's eyes narrowed at the memory. "I never saw him again."

"Were you very scared, Tatush?" I asked. I knew that I would have been.

"No, I wasn't scared. I was angry, and I was sad. This man could not see his true enemy, because he was so blinded by hatred of a Jew." He shrugged and pulled a Gauloise from the blue packet on the table, putting it between his lips. He shuffled the cards and started to deal five cards to each of us. While he dealt, he changed the topic.

"Sevek, I saw Maurice today. He's prepared to take you on as an apprentice." He paused, ran his thumb over the tip of his tongue to moisten it, and continued dealing. "You'll finish out this school year, but with the war coming, it doesn't make sense for you to return in the fall. It's a good opportunity."

Severin adjusted his glasses as he listened, staring at the cards on the table in front of him. The apprenticeship wasn't presented to Severin as a choice, as something he had the option to decline. Maurice Tsibulsky was a good friend of Papa's from Poland, an upholsterer with his own shop just down the street, and Papa had made the arrangements and the decision.

"Yes, Papa," Severin said.

"And Henek," Papa continued, looking now directly at him, in a manner that bore no argument, "you will also start as an apprentice, with me." I don't know for sure why Henri didn't go to work for one of the other craftsmen Papa knew, but I suspect that, while Father knew that he could trust Severin under someone else's supervision, he wanted to keep a closer eye on Henri.

"Sure, Papa, that sounds great," Henri said agreeably.

"What about me?" I asked.

"You will stay in school," he said. With that settled, we started the next game of belote.

While life in Paris was much the same, a lot had changed in Poland, where the bulk of our extended family still lived. Both Mama and Papa had grown up in the Jewish quarter of Warsaw, on streets where Yiddish was far more common than Polish. They were from large Orthodox families, and most of their relatives were still living in Warsaw. Now my parents read the Yiddish newspapers with renewed interest, scanning for any mention of what was happening in their home country. Each week at the cinema, Papa leaned forward in his seat when the newsreels showed footage of Warsaw, and if the voiceover was too complicated for his rudimentary French, I whispered the Yiddish translation in his ear.

By the end of November 1939, only two months after the Germans had taken Poland, the Nazis required all Polish Jews to wear an identifying white armband emblazoned with the blue Star of David. It was a seemingly innocuous omen of things to come for Jews across Europe. Each morning, as my grandmother moved the clinking glass milk bottles into her wooden cart to start her daily deliveries, she wore the armband. When my cousins played in the streets with their friends, they wore the armband. When my aunts waited in long lines at the markets, clutching their wicker baskets, they wore the armband. And when my uncles prepared to leave home, whether they were heading to work or the synagogue, they made sure the armband was prominently displayed. Sometimes it was worn high, around the biceps; other times the armband slipped down so it was like a cuff, worn near the wrist. But it was always there, and always on the right arm. So while people in Western Europe continued to refer to it as the Phony War, the period between September 1939 to April 1940 was a very real war for those in Eastern Europe.

My parents waited anxiously for news of their family back home, but mail was slow and infrequent. Madame Raymond put the mail on a small table in the courtyard, near the entrance to Stairway 1. Each day when we returned from the Marché d'Aligre, the large outdoor market on the Place d'Aligre, we were hopeful that news would be waiting.

"Anything for us, Madame Raymond?" my mother would ask.

"I'm sorry Madame Parkiet, there is nothing today," she inevitably responded sympathetically. "I'm sure there will be good news soon," she often added, though of course she had no idea.

By October 1940, Warsaw's Jewish neighborhood was sequestered: Streets that once connected to the rest of the city became dead ends, the entire area converted into a maze of false starts and walled-off passageways with only one heavily guarded way in and out. Jews lived in a neighborhood that had been converted into a prison: the Warsaw Ghetto.

These prisoners included Aunt Baltsza, who had stared in awe at the fireworks illuminating the Eiffel Tower on Bastille Day in 1937. She still lived in Warsaw with her husband, Mordechai, and their two round-faced and giggly daughters, Bronia and Halina. I never got to meet these cousins, but I can imagine what they might have been like. They were older than my brothers, and I picture them fussing over their younger cousins, brushing their hair and treating them like living dolls. Also trapped in the Warsaw Ghetto were Mama's younger sisters Rivka and Chava. In photos, Rivka had deep, serious eyes. Did she dream of moving west like my mother? Was Chava somber, or did she like to laugh? Did she enjoy sewing? Dancing? Papa had five siblings still in Warsaw: his sisters Chaya and Dwojra were there caring for their mother, Tsipi. His three brothers, Mordechai, Ytzhak, and Azriel, also lived and worked in the Polish capital. Were they varnishers like my father and grandfather? Carpenters? Was Ytzhak a musician? Was Azriel in love? Was Mordechai devout, with the long *payot* [sidelocks] of the faithful, believing in the greatness of God?

I don't know. I will never know, because not one of them survived.

In preparation for the possibility that the Germans would drop bombs of mustard gas, as happened in World War I, the French government issued gas masks to all civilians.

At school, impromptu practice drills were held so we could learn how to put the masks on quickly without help from our teachers. The mask was uncomfortable – it made your face hot and the rubber smelled horrible. With every exhale, the mask tended to push off your face with a wet, flatulent sound that, during drills, caused all of us boys to dissolve into giggles.

When the air raid sirens went off at home, our family, along with all the neighbors of Stairway 1, tromped obediently down the stairs into the cellar – *la cave*; its dark, earthy smell, with a whiff of earthworms and rotting logs. The cellar had a hard-packed dirt floor; large wooden beams served as columns and ceiling support. We stayed there, in this dank, crypt-like space, until the drill was over. The men played cards by candlelight around a table while the women sat on chairs in the opposite corner, chatting, everyone wearing a gas mask around their neck in case it was needed.

One night as we settled into the cellar, our concierge, Monsieur Raymond, turned in a circle, muttering and patting his jacket pockets. "Ah, I forgot the cards upstairs," he finally said.

My father called me over with a quick wave. "Binem, please get our deck of cards."

I was flattered that my father trusted me – the youngest of his sons, just six years old – to go upstairs on my own. I was also terrified. Me? *By myself?*

I must have looked worried because Papa leaned in and whispered, "Don't worry, it's perfectly safe. There's nothing to be afraid of."

That was easy for him to say. But everyone's eyes were on me now and I was determined to hide my nerves. I reached for a candle. Madame Nicolas, standing with Madame Raymond and my mother, a lantern in her hand, smiled at me. "*Quel jeune homme courageux* [What a brave young man]," she said, the firelight dancing in her eyes.

Holding my candle in front of me and trying very hard to keep it steady, I left the cellar and climbed the stairs slowly to prevent the flame from going out. One step. Another. After what seemed like forever I was at the ground level, and through the entrance to Stairway 1 I could see the moon's glow; it illuminated this part of the stairway and gave me a second to catch my breath. The gas mask dangled from my neck like a dead appendage and the filter canister bumped against my legs, creating an unwieldy tripping hazard. My hands were shaking and the sound of everyone talking in the cellar had faded. All I could hear was the pounding of blood in my ears. I continued up. Thump. Thump. Thump. The sound of my shoes on the stairs matched the pounding of my heart. I left behind the moonglow. Outside the candle's immediate aura was a deep, endless black, the dark of nightmares. It felt like anything could be out there, cloaked by that vast darkness: sharp claws and snarling teeth, or the bony, grasping hand of some long-dead prior resident. My mind raced ... Monsieur Dupont.

Monsieur Dupont was an elderly wraith of a man who'd lived next door until he died about a year ago. Even alive, he'd rarely emerged from his apartment, and when he did, he was silent and unsmiling in a way that I found unsettling, so I always tried to avoid encountering him. He died in his apartment, and I watched from our doorway, with my mother's arms wrapped around me, as his body, draped in a sheet, was carried down the stairs and away. Where, I wondered at the time, were they taking it?

Now, climbing the stairs, I remembered the shape of his body under the sheet and how at the time I'd wondered what his body looked like under it. I stopped on the stairs, shaking. *No, ghosts aren't real,* I told myself. *Papa said there was nothing to be afraid of.* I started up again. Right foot. Left foot. The candle created a spooky show of dancing silhouettes that it took all of my strength to ignore. I pictured the dead body of Monsieur Dupont, his skull with wide, staring eyes in the sockets, a skeleton sheathed in a black suit, covered in moss and rot, the stench of the grave. *No!* I forced the thought from my head. Right. Left. Right. I made it to the landing of the first floor and continued up, the creak of the stairs like the low whine of a demon, taunting me. Finally, I was on the second-floor landing and, my hand trembling, I opened our door.

Once inside, I snatched up the cards and bolted back out, the door slamming behind me. The door created such a clap in the otherwise silent hallway that I knew that if I hadn't awakened any monsters before, I'd surely awakened them now. I descended as quickly as I dared, the gas mask bouncing around my neck and invisible ghouls snapping at my heels, their bony, grasping fingers about to close around my throat. I almost skidded to a stop at the cellar door, and when I opened it, everyone looked up: Over a dozen friendly faces, each lit by a candle, smiled at me. I had never been so happy to see my neighbors in all my life.

Papa grinned and waved me over. The men were still standing around the card table, talking and smoking while they waited for my return. The women of Stairway 1 were in the opposite corner, perched on folding chairs. Madame Meyer, who suffered from claustrophobia in the cellar, was smiling nervously as Madame Reginaud tried to distract her with the neighborhood gossip. Madame Raymond appeared disgruntled by whatever they were talking about, and Mama nodded as she followed the conversation as best she could. Severin and Henri were laughing with René, who, handsome, self-assured, and several years older than they, was someone they admired. Madame Nicolas was smiling at me. I was even happy to see grumpy Madame Poirier and her equally grumpy husband. The monsters in my mind vanished and I handed the cards over to my father proudly, *un jeune homme courageux* indeed.

7

MAY 1940 – INVADED

"Danzig!" With that one word, spat into a microphone on May 10, 1940, the drôle de guerre ended and the real war began for us.

Danzig, a semiautonomous city-state with a much-coveted port, was sandwiched between Poland and Germany but populated almost exclusively by ethnic Germans. Located northwest of Warsaw, Danzig had belonged to the Germans until their defeat in World War I, when it became known as the Free City. Hitler wanted it back. Danzig was also the code that Hitler used to instruct Germany to invade Belgium and Holland in an effort known as *Fall Gelb* [Case Yellow]. The ultimate goal was to take Paris and, after the Germans easily took Belgium, they advanced on France.

The common belief was that France had the technologically superior army. Parisians were optimistic the fighting would be over soon. It was, but not how anyone expected. France's primary defense against Germany was a fortification called the Maginot Line. The term "line" was somewhat misleading because in truth it was more of an underground city, a complex series of bunkers that ran deep below the surface. The Maginot Line was impervious to tanks and aerial bombing and could house thousands of soldiers. The fortifications extended northward to France's borders with Luxembourg and Belgium but were notably weaker there since the French deemed an attack from that direction highly unlikely. An area of particular weakness was the Ardennes Forest, where the natural terrain and limited roads appeared to make the area impassable. It was this miscalculation that enabled Germany to invade. German soldiers slipped quietly through the forest thickets and avoided the well-prepared troops waiting for them elsewhere. France had built an impressive defense system, but the Germans sidestepped it.

The war was now on French soil. The Germans advanced on Paris and government officials fled south under the assumption the city would be bombed. Parisians followed en masse in what became known as the Exodus of Paris. Two million packed up their belongings and decamped from the city; the streets were strewn with open suitcases and boxes that had been discarded when they became too heavy to carry. Abandoned pets scrounged for food – they were all ribs and dull, flat fur.

At 5 rue de Charonne, residents gathered in the courtyard to talk about who was leaving and who was staying. Our concierges, Monsieur, and Madame Raymond, had tenants and the courtyard to look after. They collected the rent, sorted the mail, and managed the communal phone line; they were staying. The Meyers and the Reginauds weren't going anywhere either: Neither couple wanted to leave their shop. Madame Nicolas would continue working at the Prefecture de Police, or central police station. It seemed that only families with young children were evacuating so Papa made arrangements for us to leave.

My teenage brothers went to a camp in the countryside with a number of their classmates. They boarded a bus with other excited, apprehensive boys – a tangle of jostling elbows and nervous energy. Mama and I went to the Gare de Lyon train station; we were heading south to a village that had opened its doors to mothers and young children. The station buzzed with a barely contained panic, the veneer of civility worn thin by fear. My mother, standing with our battered suitcase resting between her feet, was nervous. She didn't like crowds. She held onto me firmly, almost too tightly, with one hand. In the other, she clutched a familiar talisman: her beloved locket, a gift from my father nine years before.

When my father emigrated from Warsaw, he knew that he would not see his wife for a long time. Before he had boarded the train, he pulled a small object from his suit jacket and pressed it into her palm. "I don't want you to forget what I look like," he said. He held my mother's hands; they were an island of quiet in the chaos of the train station. Around them, newsboys shouted out the dismal headlines of the *Kurier Warszawski*, the local paper, and Polska Roma sang sorrowful melodies in the gray corridors of the depot. Mama turned her palm over and examined the locket he'd placed there; on one side was a mirror, on the other a sepia portrait of Papa wearing a fine suit and an earnest expression. "Yosel, I love it." Her blue eyes sparkled with tears. He touched her cheek.

"Don't worry, I will send for you soon."

Now, nine years later, the family was once again separating. Her older boys were off with their classmates, her husband was working away in his shop, and this time it was she who was leaving, with me. Gare de Lyon was loud; everyone was chattering, and almost anything – a shout, a shove – would have been enough to break what remained of the fragile decorum. We began to be jostled along in the crowds, pushed toward the train. Mama bent to pick up our suitcase, and as she did, the locket fell from her hand and was swiftly kicked away by the many moving feet.

"Binem – my locket!" she screamed. We scanned the ground frantically, trying to catch a glimpse of silver as feet stepped around us. There were so many shoes: black and brown, big and small, shiny and dull. Cigarette butts and other litter made it hard to see anything. Was that the locket? No, it was a discarded candy wrapper, the foil shining like gold. There were hundreds of people, all carrying suitcases and satchels. How were we to find it? To get any closer to the ground was to risk being trampled. No, the locket was gone and Mama was not willing to miss our train to keep searching. As we claimed our seats, my mother looked out of the window, still hoping to see it on the ground.

I knew how much that locket meant to Mama. She never went anywhere without it. "I'm sorry, Mama," I said.

She patted my hand. "It's all right, Binem, at least I did not lose you."

As the train rattled through the fields outside the city, the sound of airplanes and bombs in the distance mingled with the quiet sighs of my mother. Losing the locket seemed like bad luck, not a good way to start our trip.

The village's administrative buildings had been taken over for temporary housing, so we were directed to a red-and-white brick schoolhouse where we were assigned adjacent metal cots, two of the 50 or so that were organized into rows in the large room. The wooden school desks, which were covered in the pocketknife scratches of the village's young residents, had been pushed into a corner and stacked in precarious towers. A chalkboard was used by the administrators to communicate general information, which I translated for my mother. After a day or two, the chalk was moved to another room for safekeeping, the authorities having realized it was unwise to leave so much unsupervised chalk around so many unoccupied, prankish children.

The country smelled like the color green, of grass and hay, and sometimes of manure. I went barefoot for the first time and the bottoms of my feet quickly grew calloused. The rest of me turned golden from the sun.

There were snails everywhere and I collected them, stuffing my pockets with my new friends. Sometimes at night the snails were lucky enough to escape, leaving a slimy trail across the wood floor. More often they were discovered by my mother as she gathered my discarded clothes; she was less than enamored of the squishy surprises I'd left her.

At some point, it became clear that the Germans were not going to bomb Paris, and Mama grew restless. She watched as other mothers began departing to head back to Paris until one day she announced, "Binem, we are going to go home tomorrow. I'm sure you miss your father. I know I do." She was hanging laundry on a line. I stood near her and handed her clothespins one at a time. I wore the clothespins clamped on my left hand like porcupine needles, enjoying the relief of removing them and noticing the pinched red marks they left on my hands.

"Really? Are you sure we should go back?" I asked. I did miss my father. I missed Titi, too. But I was enjoying the countryside and the new experiences. I moved away from her to stand on a rail of the horse paddock and tried to lure a nearby gelding to come nibble at my right, non-porcupined hand. The farther I leaned over the fence in his direction, the more he danced away, his glossy coat shimmering, his tail swishing in disdain.

The next day a police car, shiny and beetle black, picked us up to take us back to the train station. "Have you ever ridden in a police car before?" the gendarme asked me as I clambered in after my mother.

"No, sir, I've never even ridden in a taxi!"

"Well, stay out of trouble and hopefully you'll never have to ride in one again," he joked.

I bounced on the leather seat and rolled the window up and down, up and down, under the indulgent gaze of the gendarme who smiled at me from the rearview window until my distracted mother put a hand on my leg. I leaned out the open window to take great gulping breaths of the air I was leaving behind.

As we approached the station, I felt my mother stiffen. She sat up straight. "Yosel?" It was a whispered question. Then, "*Mon mari! Mon mari* [My husband! My husband]!" and she thrust her arm out the open car window, pointing at something in the distance.

I followed her arm. There was the familiar shape of my father in his trench coat and trilby hat, standing outside of the train station, a cigarette in his hand. The police car pulled up and Mama and I leapt out. I ran to my father and pressed my face into his clothes, inhaling the scent of varnish.

"What are you doing here? Is everything okay?" she asked.

Now it was Papa's turn to be surprised and his brow furrowed in confusion as he squinted at us. "Rikla? Binem? How did you know I was coming?"

"I could ask you the same question. And we didn't know. We were coming home," Mama said.

My father laughed. "And I was coming to get both of you! Now that we know that the Germans aren't going to bomb Paris, it's safe to come home again."

I looked up at my father, then at my mother, my gaze alternating between them in my utter delight that we were all together again. The world was as it was supposed to be.

Why did my parents marry? I remember asking my father back when I was a young boy watching him work in his workshop. I was sitting cross-legged and the floor was covered in a fine sawdust that I would bring back home with me. "Papa, how did you know you were going to marry Mama? Did you always know?" I could not imagine a time that they weren't together, but equally, I could not imagine them young and in love in the ways I'd seen in the movies. "Did Mama always love you? Did you always love her?"

He paused in his work, appearing to weigh his answer carefully. "Well, you know we grew up in the same neighborhood, so we knew of each other," he said. "We may have had friends in common, we passed in the streets, but we didn't really talk to each other." He bent again, his face to the table, and focused on a particular nick in the table, intent on sanding it away.

"I was very different back then," he continued. "I spent a lot of time in the synagogue. I had long payot, like the men we see in the Pletzel [Jewish quarter in the 4th arrondissement], and I dressed in black like them. I spent all day praying and studying the Torah."

I tried to imagine Papa with the long curls that I saw on other Jewish men in the Pletzel. The men with the long beards who wore black suits even in the heat of summer.

"She wanted a man of the world, not a man of God." My father blew the dust from where he'd been sanding and straightened up again, and I heard the percussive crack of his spine as he stretched. "When I came back from serving in the military, I had short hair and I suppose I looked more like the sort of man she wanted to marry. The shadchan [matchmaker] introduced us."

It was a good match. Father was passionate, quick-tempered, and driven. He needed someone like my mother, gentle, quiet, and capable of providing calm amid the tornado of his energy. On April 4, 1924, they were married under the chuppah in the Nożyk Synagogue.

I don't remember seeing my parents hug or kiss each other. Typical of the times, they were not prone to romantic displays. But the matchmaker had indeed chosen well: It was a true partnership. Romantic love is, after all, a relatively modern construct and until recently was reserved for the very wealthy. Who else had time for such frivolity? Despite their less-than-poetic introduction, my parents loved each other deeply, and they were connected in powerful ways.

Now we stood outside the train station, reveling in our unexpected reunion, and the sense of providence and destiny it carried.

"Well then," Papa said, clapping his hands together, "I suppose we can go inside and wait for the next train home!"

"Where are Henek and Sevek?" my mother asked.

"Still at camp. I tried to get them, but they are having so much fun that they didn't want to come home yet. Don't worry," he said, patting my mother's hand. "I will get them soon, but why not let them enjoy the country while they can?" My father took our suitcase from my mother.

On the train home I watched as the trees that lined the train tracks flew by, a green blur. The clouds, puffy and cotton white, kept pace with us, as if accompanying us on our journey home. Gradually the world in the window turned from green to gray, with tall trees replaced by even taller buildings. My mother, her eyes moist and sorrowful, told my father that she'd lost the locket.

Once we pulled into Gare de Lyon, we went to the station office to see if the locket had been turned in by someone. The station agent, a sallow man with a narrow wisp of a mustache, pulled a box from the floor. He rooted through the wooden crate, moving a scarf aside, a monogrammed lighter, a child's red woolen glove with a thread trailing like a tail from its cuff. And there it was, the little mirror with my father's face on one side. The agent held the locket up and compared the photo with my father. "Looks like you all right," he said with a squint.

"It's a miracle!" my mother repeated, shaking her head and smiling. "*Merci,* Monsieur!" She took the locket, cradling it in her hands briefly, and then placed it back in the safety of her purse, patting it on the side. For that brief moment in time, life looked hopeful.

"It's not that easy to get rid of me, Rikla," Papa said with a wink, and we went home.

On the morning of June 14, 1940, just one month after the German army first set foot on French soil, the Nazis took Paris. Throughout the city the sounds of a German-accented voice boomed through a loudspeaker, advising in French that a curfew would be in effect that night as the Wehrmacht arrived. By evening, soldiers marched through the empty streets, followed by slow-rolling tanks.

In the provisional capital of Vichy, the French leadership argued. The government was split. Some wanted to fall back to the French colonies in Africa and continue the fight from there. The French had a powerful navy, so it was possible. Others felt they could not abandon the remaining French citizens and had to reach some sort of agreement with the Germans. The latter path won the day, and in July, 84-year-old Marshal Philippe Pétain, a World War I war hero with a white walrus mustache and a reassuringly paternal countenance, took the helm of the new French government, called Vichy France. With the establishment of the Vichy regime, Pétain replaced the French motto of *Liberté, Égalité, Fraternité* [Freedom, Equality, Brotherhood] with *Travail, Famille, Patrie* [Work, Family, Homeland]. The repudiation of the motto of the French Republic could not be misconstrued; it represented a deliberate withdrawal from its aspirational values.

When Germany was vanquished in World War I, the armistice was signed 80 kilometers north of Paris in the Forest of Compiègne in a railway car that had served as a mobile command center for Marshal Ferdinand Foch, the French general who was the Allied commander-in-chief. For the 1940 armistice, Hitler ordered the same railway car, known as the Compiègne Car, moved back to the exact location of the 1918 signing, and he sat in the same seat that the victorious French marshal had occupied in 1918. The next day, Hitler went on a whirlwind tour of the main tourist sites of Paris, not even stopping to take a meal. It was the only time he visited Paris, and he departed for Berlin right after posing for a photo in front of the Eiffel Tower.

Despite the armistice, not all French military were ready to admit defeat. Charles de Gaulle, then a newly promoted brigadier general, decamped for London once it was clear that Pétain intended to concede. De Gaulle was a tall and imperious man with a prominent nose set in a hound dog face; at six feet, five inches tall, he looked down on most of the people around him, literally as well as figuratively. On June 18, 1940, while the Germans were still settling into Paris, de Gaulle addressed France from London with a microphone provided by British Prime Minister Winston Churchill. In the first of what would be many communications via the BBC, de Gaulle urged the French to keep fighting and to keep the spirit of resistance alive. While only a few French people heard the broadcast, it is often considered the start of the French Resistance and also of the Free French, the government-in-exile that de Gaulle would come to lead.

With the German occupation, the split character of France was revealed. Pétain had settled; de Gaulle was off fighting. What, who, was France now? In Paris, most people chose to flee or concede. Wealthy Jews left for other parts of the world, having seen what Hitler had done to Jews in Germany. But we did not leave because, like many recent immigrants, we were not wealthy and had nowhere to go. And there was the rest of the family to think about. Aunt Maryla was still in Brussels, but Belgium had already fallen to the Germans. Everyone else was still in Poland, and Poland was under German control. Most importantly, we had no reason to believe that life would be any better anywhere else we could go. So we did the only thing we could: We watched, waited, and hoped for the best.

It wasn't that bad at the beginning. The cafés reopened and were filled with celebratory German soldiers. In those early days, they were in general polite and pleasant occupiers, doffing their hats to women, offering their Métro seats to the elderly. Many of the Parisians who'd fled south returned, trickling back to the city as reports reached them that it was safe.

Paris adopted a tentative peace, but the economy – and our finances – suffered. Many of Papa's regular clients were not placing orders; Parisians who'd only recently packed their bags were unlikely to invest in a pair of matching taborets for their sitting room. Monsieur Tsibulsky had no need for an apprentice, and Papa could not teach Henri when there was no furniture to refinish.

With an immigrant's spirit of improvisation, my father found new work. He purchased small silver-plated replicas of famous Parisian landmarks from a wholesaler in the 4th arrondissement, lugging the wooden boxes of trinkets home on the crowded Métro. At night, he and my brothers assembled cardboard boxes to house the miniature replicas, stacking them in towers on our dining table, and each morning they took the Métro east to the Château de Vincennes. The Germans had converted part of the medieval fortress, originally a hunting lodge for Louis VII, into barracks. It now housed the Wehrmacht, the army foot soldiers, regular German boys who had been conscripted into serving their country. Papa, Severin, and Henri stood outside the bridge that went over the massive dry moat and greeted the Wehrmacht as they passed by.

"Excuse me, *mein Herr,* might I interest you in a souvenir?" Papa would ask. "When you go home to your mother or your girlfriend, perhaps you'd like to bring home a bit of Paris to show her what you've seen and where you've been."

Papa's Yiddish allowed him to talk to the soldiers almost fluently; in fact, it was easier for Papa to speak with Germans than it was to communicate with our own neighbors. And my father bore these young men no ill will: They didn't necessarily adhere to any antisemitic ideology, they were merely serving their country as they'd been instructed. Interactions were usually friendly and good-natured.

At night, while they prepared for the next workday, my brothers told stories of the day's adventures. One afternoon, a soldier purchased a replica of the Eiffel Tower, the tallest statue we sold. He tried to close the box, but the tower was too tall. The soldier, a curl of his slick-backed hair loose and dangling over one eye, tried to force the lid down. He blew the hair out of his eye and pushed, and the statue pierced the lid.

Papa, Severin, Henri, and the soldier all looked at the little Eiffel Tower and laughed. The spire peaked out like the head of a baby bird breaking through its egg.

"Well, sir," my father joked, "it seems that the tower cannot be contained. It is after all the tallest building in all of Europe, almost the world."

The soldier laughed, my father laughed – everyone laughed. France may have been an occupied nation and things were different, but everyone was getting along just fine.

Titi and I could hear them coming from blocks away. Then at the corner of rue de Charonne and rue du Faubourg Saint-Antoine, we saw them. The *Feldgendarmerie*. Their legs moved in unison like scissors, slicing through the air with mechanical efficiency; their shiny black boots clapped down like advancing thunder. No soldier was out of order, none less than perfect: they were one creature with many legs. This was a far cry from the pimply-faced Wehrmacht. This was Hitler's military police, also known as the *Kettenhunde* [Chain Dogs], because of the metal gorgets on their chests. The crescent-shaped pieces of armor, decorated with a bright gold Nazi eagle, hung from the steel linked chain that circled their necks; the gorgets glinted in the afternoon sun, rising and falling with each step, hitting the soldier's chests in unison with the clang of a cymbal.

Everyone gathered on the streets to watch them go by: White-aproned shopkeepers left their stores, boys on bicycles pulled over, and mothers clutched their young children to their side. Walking home from school, Titi and I stopped and watched in silence as they passed us. The Feldgendarmerie had faces of stone; they appeared completely unaware of us, indifferent to our presence. It was as if they sensed some of their power lay in their utter disregard for whatever was going on around them.

It was impossible not to be impressed. After they passed, Titi and I marched home in imitation of the Feldgendarmerie, our legs straight in front of us, our arms at our side. We fixed our eyes into a flinty stare and stomped back and forth in the courtyard, pivoting as a single unit until the sun went behind the buildings. We marched past the departing workers who, backs stooped with fatigue, were heading home. We patrolled the perimeter of the courtyard, trying our best to be intimidating and remote. We made our faces into stone, not acknowledging Monsieur Sherapan when he shuffled by and waved in greeting. The sun slipped behind the western buildings of the courtyard and yet we marched onward. We were impassive and mechanical when Madame Nicolas returned from the Prefecture de Police and headed up Stairway 1, a bemused smile on her face as she watched our procession. We marched until I heard my father call me home from the open apartment window. "Binem, *Aroyf in shteeb!*" he shouted, Yiddish for "Binem, come up home." René, leaning against an exterior wall and talking with his sister Paulette, raised his eyebrows and smiled at me. "Binem, Aroyf in shteeb," he echoed, the Yiddish phrase familiar to him though he did not understand it. Titi and I nodded at each other as we silently agreed to part, and Titi stomped off toward Stairway 3. René saluted me as I marched past him on my way into Stairway 1 and I couldn't help but grin back at him, knees high as I mounted the stairs, a soldier on his way home to supper.

It may seem odd that instead of being afraid I was excited by what I'd seen, but I was only seven, and did not yet know enough to be afraid of Nazi soldiers. We should have been terrified but, as we were soon to learn, it was the French police, our own gendarmerie, we most needed to fear.

Photo of Yosel (Joseph) in a locket

8

AUGUST 1941 – DETAINED

On Wednesday, August 20, 1941, Papa rose around 7 a.m. Mama was already back from the boulangerie, and Papa sipped a cup of sugared tea with his bread and butter. He read the front page of the Yiddish newspaper while absentmindedly dabbing up breadcrumbs with his index finger. At approximately 8 a.m., after his morning cigarette, he strolled across the courtyard, humming as he climbed the stairs to his workshop. He shook shellac flakes into a mason jar and poured alcohol over them, the shellac dissolving into swirling brown ribbons until the resulting varnish was a murky brown, the color of the Seine.

My father's workday was just beginning, but the gendarmerie of Paris had been hard at work for hours. They started blocking streets out of the 11th arrondissement at 5 a.m.; by 6 a.m. they'd closed all the Métro entrances. By 8:30, as my father smoothed the first coat of varnish onto a writing desk, hundreds of Jewish men, ages 16 to 50, had been detained by the police. At the end of the day, the number would be over 4,000.

In the late morning, there was a knock at the front door, and Severin, alone in the apartment, opened it to find two caped gendarmes.

One of them looked at a piece of paper in his hands. "We are looking for Issahar Parkiet. Iss-a-SHA? Also, Joseph Parkiet. Are you Joseph or Iss-a-SHA?"

Issahar was Severin's Hebrew name, his formal, legal name; it was the name on his identity papers. No one used it. He was Sevek to my parents, and Severin to Henri, me, and everyone else in Paris. Even back in Poland, his family never addressed him as Issahar. His heart sped.

"I do not know an Issahar; there is no one here by that name," he lied. "Joseph is my father, but he is at work."

Frowning at the paper, the gendarme scratched the name Issahar off the list. Then, in the rote and emotionless manner of someone who has said the same phrase hundreds of times, he said, "When Joseph Parkiet gets home, he must come to the police station. Someone needs to accompany him. And tell him that he should not think about disobeying this order. If he does not appear, it will mean trouble for the entire family."

"Yes, of course," Severin nodded. His heart was in his throat now as if it wanted to leap out of his mouth and run away, It was pounding so loudly that he feared the police would hear it and know he was lying. He was 16 years old, small for his age, and while his hands were calloused from his year as an upholsterer's apprentice, his cheeks still bore the youthful flush of acne. Severin did not tell them my father's work was just across the courtyard, only steps away. He did not tell them that, in under a minute, they could be hammering on Joseph Parkiet's workshop door.

The gendarmes turned away and continued up the stairs to the fourth floor. Severin listened with the door cracked as they delivered the same stern message to our upstairs neighbor, Monsieur Adler.

"Why do I need to come? What is it exactly that needs to be sorted out?" Monsieur Adler asked. His voice had a desperate, almost childish, insistence – the voice was of someone trying to maintain dignity in the face of absolute authority despite rising fear. It was strange to hear that from an adult.

"There is an issue with your identity papers, and it must be sorted out at the station," a gendarme said. "If your papers are in order, there is nothing to worry about."

Why would you disobey when you had done nothing wrong? Who wanted to risk trouble with the police? Who wanted to make trouble for their family? Only the guilty, only those with something to hide, would consider disobeying.

Severin listened as three sets of footsteps walked down the stairs, then he ran to the courtyard window and watched as Monsieur Adler, wedged between the gendarmes, left the courtyard clutching a small bag to his chest. Once they were gone, Severin bolted to Papa's workshop.

Mama, Henri and I were home from the market by the time Severin returned with Papa. She was chopping onions in preparation for supper and Henri was building a wooden model ship at the table while I watched, my feet swinging back and forth beneath the chair. I badly wanted to help, but Henri wouldn't let me, so I sat on my hands to keep them from touching anything.

Papa explained that he needed to go to the police station to sort out something regarding his identity papers. "Do not worry, I'll be home soon. After all, I've done nothing wrong. Henek, why don't you come with me? There is no reason to risk the police asking Sevek more questions."

An hour later, Henri returned alone, upset. "They wouldn't tell me anything," he said, near tears, and Mama put her arms around him. Papa had been detained, and Henri was only home to pick up some things for him – a blanket and one day's worth of clothes and food.

Where was he being taken? Why? When would he be allowed to come home? Was there something we could do? Henri had no answers to our questions because the police had not answered his. All he could report was that Papa said it would be fine, not to worry. Papa was sure he would be home in a day or so once everything was straightened out.

I know now that, from the police station, Papa was taken to another location in the 11th arrondissement, the Japy gymnasium. There he stood in the large echoing room with other Jews, men he knew from the neighborhood – including Monsieur Adler – trying to guess what was happening. The competing sounds of Yiddish and French ricocheted off the walls; some men were worried, talking about what little they knew of events in Poland, but most were confident that the detention would be brief. They had done nothing wrong.

Hours passed with no information; the floor was covered with discarded cigarette butts, like a smattering of dirty snow. The air grew thick with the smell of sweat and tobacco: Jackets were removed, sleeves rolled up, and everything wrinkled in the moist, warm room. The gym became a tropical terrarium; the high windows were foggy, the condensation building up and resolving into beads that left streaky trails as they descended. The sun, heavy and low, turned the room orange. When the sun descended below the windows, twilight gave the gym a blue, gloomy hue and the men grew tired of standing; they sat on the gymnasium floor, kneading their satchels into pillows. Eventually, fatigued and with rumbling stomachs, they were herded onto a Paris city bus and taken 16 kilometers northeast to the suburb of Drancy.

A squeal of brakes and the buses stopped. The rumble of the diesel engine died: Here they would get off. Papa had arrived at *La Cité de la Muette*, or The Silent City. It would soon be known as the Drancy camp, the main French gateway to Auschwitz.

9

SEPTEMBER 1941 – PILES OF STOLEN RADIOS

On Thursday, August 28, 1941, I turned eight, quietly and without ceremony. Papa had been gone for a week with no news. A few days later, as we argued over who could control the radio – Henri smacked my hand away as I tried to turn the dial – we froze at the word *Juifs* [Jews] coming from the speaker. Mama, a soapy plate in her hand, turned toward the radio so suddenly that the heel of one of her shoes squeaked. Her French was poor, but that was a word she knew well.

Une ordonnante du Militarbefelhlshaber en France vient de décider que les Juifs, résidant en territoire occupé n'auront plus le droit d'avoir en leur possession des appareils de T.S.F. Ils devront remettre leurs appareils récepteurs aux Commissaires de police qui leur en délivreront reçu. Cette mesure a été rendure nécessaire par le fait que des Juifs répandaient dans le public les fausses nouvelles émises par certains postes étrangers.

"Sevek?" my mother asked, needing translation.

In the last week, Severin had adopted the stoic but sorrowful stance of the reluctant man of the house. "We have to give up our radio," he said. "The Germans have said that Jews are no longer allowed to own radios because Jews have been spreading lies."

"That's ridiculous!" Henri said. "They can't make us do that!" He stood from the table, indignant. When neither Severin or Mama spoke, he wilted, his bravado gone. "Can they make us do that?" His voice quavered, and in his question I heard the confusion that I was feeling.

45

It was Severin who had the idea. We had to turn in a radio, but it didn't have to be ours. "I'll go see Madame Raymond," he said.

"I'm coming too," Henri said.

"Me too!" I echoed, not wanting to be left behind.

We went to see our concierge, tromping down the stairs in single file, the radio under Severin's arm. When we found her, she was sorting the day's mail, organizing it into separate stacks for each tenant.

We offered her a trade: her radio for ours. We would turn hers over to the police. La Pipelette had an old radio with a long crack running like a river down the side as if it had been accidentally dropped. It crackled when you turned the dial, and all the voices sounded like they were coming from an underground tunnel. Our radio was new and the sound was crisp and clear.

At first, she demurred. "No, I can't. Yours is so much nicer."

"But if you don't take it, the police will. And we would much rather that you have it." Severin pressed it forward.

"Well, I certainly do not want those *Boches* [derogatory term for German soldiers] to have it," Madame Raymond tutted, and she reluctantly accepted the gift. The Vichy government had issued the mandate, but everyone knew the Germans were behind it. She retrieved her radio, wiping off a thin layer of dust before handing it to us. A tall woman, she bent down to look at me with her massive caterpillar brows wiggling. A few wisps of her black hair had escaped her bun, giving her a frizzy halo. She smiled at me and said, "You must come listen to the radio whenever you want."

As a very young boy, I'd been terrified of our concierge; I frequently hid behind my mother's dress when we encountered her, peeking out to catch a glimpse. As I grew older, I recognized Madame Raymond's gruff exterior for what it was: the only line of defense in the protection of her tender heart. Still, she remained intimidating and I was not alone in being cowed by her: I suspected her wisp of a husband was similarly frightened given the docile way he followed her around. There was no doubt who was in charge in their home.

My brothers and I walked to the 11th arrondissement police station, around the corner from my school. Henri had insisted on accompanying Severin ("I want to glare at these *crétins* when we do this," he declared), and naturally, I wanted to join them. Once there, we waited in a line that curved out the door and into the street. Some people cradled their radio as if it was a newborn, others sat it at their feet like a piece of old luggage that belonged to someone else. In line in front of us was a young man, just a few years older than Severin, who stood quietly with his hands in his pockets, rocking back and forth on his heels. He didn't have a radio and he was clearly by himself, silent and brooding. I wondered why he was there.

There were more gendarmes than usual at the prefecture. They milled about, talking among themselves as radios were handed over. "They're probably waiting until we're all gone, and then they'll pick through them for themselves. That's stealing," Henri whispered furiously. And maybe they were. There were dozens of radios stacked behind the guard's desk piled on top of one another. More than enough for each gendarme to have his pick.

Henri spent the time in line guessing which of the gendarmes was most likely to steal a radio, and like a matchmaker, he guessed which radio each gendarme would pick. "That one," he said, nodding toward a plump policeman with inordinately large ears, "is desperate to go out with the receptionist, but she wants nothing to do with him. He's got his eyes on the Victrola and plans to give it to her as a gift. But she still won't go out with him because his breath smells of sauerkraut and he has ears like an elephant. 'What would our children look like?' she'll say to her friends." His voice was a falsetto as he imitated the young woman typing at a nearby desk. Henri was only a year younger than Severin, but whether due to a naturally high-spirited temperament or because he benefited from having escaped the responsibility that inevitably falls to the eldest child, he was most comfortable on the cusp of causing trouble. He was drawn toward the provocative in the way a car in need of alignment pulls toward one side of the road.

"Shhh. Shut up," Severin whispered.

We were almost at the front of the line and watched as the young man with no radio reached the gendarmes. He licked his thin lips and pulled a small object out of his pocket. I leaned forward to see it. It was a pencil sharpener shaped like a radio, the paint rubbed off the edges to reveal the die-cast metal underneath. He presented it to the police with great solemnity. And then he turned and walked away.

The gendarme held the pencil sharpener between his thumb and forefinger, inspecting it, and laughed. He tossed it to a colleague, who, chuckling, tossed it to another policeman after he'd had a look. I laughed too, a nervous titter. It was our turn now, and we handed over La Pipelette's radio. I had to stand on my tiptoes to peer over the guard's desk, and I watched as he turned the radio in his hands to look it over and then plunked it down on top of another one.

We felt weighed down on our return trip despite having nothing to carry. At home, our supper table was quiet. Over the last couple of weeks we'd done our best to find out what was going on with Father, but little information was available. Mama heard that if we went to Drancy, we might be able to glimpse him through the fence, perhaps even pass him some food. She wrapped bread and sausage in a cloth, and she and Severin took the train to Drancy. They tried for hours to find Papa among the thousands of men staring out from the tall windows, but it was impossible and they left disappointed.

Before he'd been taken, it was my habit to listen for my father's arrival home at the end of his workday. I could hear him as he climbed the spiral stairway; I knew it was him by the specific shuffle of his shoes scraping the steps, like sandpaper on wood. Each evening he pulled a chair from the table and sat down across from me, extending hands which were covered in a thick brown coat of dried lacquer. I peeled the strips off him as though they were taffy and, while I worked, he inspected my progress. Eyebrow arched, thin lips in his slightly crooked smile. I looked forward to the ritual each day.

"I think you missed a spot there," he would say, pointing, and I'd peel the piece and add it to the pile of varnish strips that curled on the table like a discarded skin. I continued my work until Papa held his vein-rippled hands out, appraising my effort, and pronounced it good. He then picked up a brush and a pumice stone and scoured the remaining bits off, humming softly, until his hands were perfectly clean.

I still listened for him each evening, but I never heard the telltale sound of his shuffle and he never came up our stairs. We no longer played cards in the evenings because without Father we could not play belote. There were no stories of life back in Poland. And now, with no radio, there was no music, no news, and our house grew quieter still, like a tomb.

That night in my fold-out bed, with the sounds of Paris coming through my mother's open window, I thought of the young man with the pencil sharpener. At eight I was not able to fully comprehend the scope of what had occurred, but I was old enough to register the young man's actions as an act of defiance. I understood that he was not Jewish, but that he was standing in solidarity with the Jews to demonstrate his disapproval of what was being done to our family, to people like us. I knew that if my father had been there, he would have been impressed. My father was a man of principles, and he admired others who stood up for their beliefs.

I missed my father. The reality of his absence crashed over me like a wave, almost violently, flooding me from the inside out. It was a physical ache, the sort of bone-deep loneliness that comes only in the middle of the night. I could sense rather than hear the soft breathing of my brothers; outside, a couple walked by and I could hear snatches of their conversation.

Other people were living their lives, still whole and complete, while our life had been upended: The center of our family had been stolen from us. I wondered where my father was, what he was doing, and when he would come home. It did not occur to me that he might not come home. We did not know until later just how bad it was.

10

THE NOOSE TIGHTENS

When my father arrived at Drancy at the end of that first interminable day, he and the other men stumbled bleary-eyed out of the buses. They entered through an open gate, surrounded by a three-meter-high double-barbed wire fence. As they walked through, the gendarmes took their ration cards. This was the first indication that they were not going to be leaving any time soon.

Papa was haphazardly prodded along with the others into one of five unfinished concrete structures, known as blocks. Each building was four stories high; the men made their way up the stairs into one of the large rooms that branched off at each landing. The rooms were open and irregularly shaped. There was no electricity, so they navigated together in the dark as if struck by a collective blindness. Few rooms had furniture, so the internees used the bundles of clothes they'd brought to form makeshift beds on the uneven, unfinished floors. They slept fitfully. Many had been detained without the knowledge of their families and were desperate to get in touch with them.

When the gray light of morning came, the internees stood and stretched, sore from sleeping on the floor. They peered through the inward-facing windows into a U-shaped complex that surrounded a courtyard. The courtyard was immense: 200 by 40 meters. The buildings were part of an unfinished apartment complex. Construction had started in 1931 but ground to a halt when money ran out during the Depression, leaving the structures an incomplete shell. Sewer pipes were visible in the floors. The outward-facing windows were boarded up. The Germans did not want internees seeing out into the neighborhood, and they did not want French citizens seeing in. SS Capt. Theodor Dannecker, who had been sent to France to oversee its anti-Jewish policies, imposed the rules. The internees were permitted to leave their block for one hour a day to exercise in the courtyard. Smoking anywhere, at any time, was strictly prohibited.

That day, Thursday, August 21, they were joined by more men. There now were a total of 5,000 internees crowded into buildings that had been designed to house, when completed, 700. Buildings had toilets but they were no more than decorative: the plumbing was unfinished and soon the toilets were overflowing. The only functional latrine was at one end of the courtyard, a small building shared by all internees. At some point, bales of hay arrived, were broken up and strewn about the floors; now the men slept on a dusting of straw, like animals in a barn.

For the first three days, there was no food.

In general, hygiene conditions at the camp were horrible and within a week the men were scratching at fleas and lice. A week later and they no longer cared about bugs, as they were too worried about starving. Hunger, and the thought of food, dominated conversation and thoughts. It was a raging hole in their stomachs, demanding attention, angry at being ignored and blocking thoughts of anything else. Papa, like all of the internees, began to waste away. He traded his silver pocket watch, a gift from his deceased father, for a ration of bread.

Next came the rule that Jews were not permitted to own bicycles. In September, two gendarmes appeared at our apartment to inspect our bicycle and announced they would return in 30 minutes to claim it.

Henri was furious. "It seems every time these *cretins* show up at our door, they take something that doesn't belong to them."

Because Vichy France collaborated with our German occupiers, the French police acted as agents of Nazi Germany. The gendarmes looked the same – the familiar blue uniforms did not change between World War I and World War II – but the men wearing them behaved differently. While there were exceptions, most gendarmes in 1941 assumed a gruff and imperious manner when interacting with Jews. It seemed a century since the policeman had watched over Henri when he was lost at the World Fair. That gendarme, the one who placed his kepi on my brother's head, whose wide thumb had wiped tears from Henri's cheek, was he now hauling away bicycles? Had he arrested men like my father? Had he thrust his palm, hard and insistent, into the back of a Jewish man to prod him into a bus destined for Drancy?

Henri got to work on the bike with a screwdriver. First, the bell came off, then the light. The bike rack fell to the floor with a metallic thunk. When the police returned, the bicycle was stripped. One of them nodded his approval. "You were smart. Other people gave us everything." What a thing, to be complimented by the person who is, under the guise of law, stealing your property. The gendarme hefted Henri's bicycle over his shoulder, the back wheel spinning as he walked out. Henri slammed the door after him and collapsed, crying hot angry tears into his grease-stained hands.

The antisemitic restrictions came quickly now. Shortly after the bicycles were taken, a curfew was imposed: Jews were not permitted outside their homes between 8 p.m. and 5 a.m. Next, we were prohibited from visiting public parks. The cinema. Cafés. The library. It was hard to keep up with the prohibitions, they were happening so fast. Mama could shop only in certain stores, and only during a narrow late-afternoon window. By the time Jewish shoppers were permitted to visit the stores, the best food was long gone; the bins might hold a few scabby onions or the sloughed-off detritus of whatever wilted greens had been snatched up hours ago.

Because two of our French neighbors were shop owners and kind, we fared better than most. Whenever we walked into the Reginauds' épicerie, Madame Reginaud surreptitiously pulled out something they'd set aside – a wedge of cheese or whatever few hardy vegetables had made their way to the shop.

"Perfect timing, Madame Parkiet," Madame Reginaud would say, revealing the day's offerings. "Today I have some cabbage" – she lifted the pale green ball – "a little bit of cheese" – she held up a small hunk of gruyère – "and, of course, milk." She stressed each item's French name (chou, du fromage, le lait) as she held it up, perpetually optimistic that my mother's mastery of the language was improving.

We depended largely on the Meyers' charcuterie for whatever meat we ate, entering through the courtyard entrance rather than the main entrance on rue de Charonne, walking past the dwindling supply of cured meats that dangled on chains from the ceiling. Monsieur Meyer always had something saved for us when Mama peeked inside. He'd pass a brown packet to his daughter silently, and she'd ring it up with a shy smile. Our neighbors were only too happy to flout the regulations imposed by the German occupiers and the French Vichy collaborators. The courtyard took care of its own.

In September, Jews were restricted to the last car on the Métro. The single car was almost always packed; there was no room to sit, and people pressed against each other in a grim portent of what was to come. Our world gradually became smaller and more constricted, a slowly tightening noose.

After the first several weeks without my father, we were permitted to send care packages. The weather grew cooler, so Mama knitted socks and gloves to keep Papa warm. My brothers and I rolled cigarettes to send to Papa, the tobacco flakes sticking to our fingers. We did not know that smoking was prohibited at Drancy, that we were spending money and time to provide cigarettes to Papa's guards. We sent the packages through the Red Cross, my father's name written on them in Severin's careful, precise script.

"How do we know that these will reach Papa?" Severin asked.

"We don't," Mama replied, her small hands moving deftly as she knitted, the soft clink of the metal needles like the tick of a clock. "But we can hope that they do." We had not expected him to be gone this long.

I fiddled with one of the cigarettes, putting it to my mouth in jest.

"That's not for you!" Severin smacked my hand away from my mouth with force, and he put the cigarette in the box.

After she made our lunch, Mama took the train to deliver the care package, leaving us at home. While she was gone, I made myself a cigarette, taking a piece of newspaper and rolling Papa's tobacco into it. The newspaper ink stuck to my fingers, leaving black smudge marks. I put my cigarette between my lips and lit it, taking a deep breath so the smoke burned my lungs. I coughed, but I felt good: older, more mature. My head tingled as if it was expanding; it grew lighter and I felt like I was rising, like a hot air balloon. Like I might float away. Tilting my chair back, as I'd seen my father do many times before, I attempted to blow smoke rings, but the smoke I exhaled was insubstantial, a stratus that disappeared into nothing within seconds.

I sat back up in the chair and smacked my lips; my mouth felt dry and woolen. My first cigarette had made me thirsty, so I stood to pick up the bottle of red wine that always sat on the floor next to the sink, gathering dust between guests. Cigarette in one hand, the bottle in the other, my head a buzzing hive from the tobacco, I grabbed the wine and took a large, inexpert gulp. Before I could even consider a second swig, my stomach roiled and everything came back up. I vomited it all, wine and lunch spewing on the floor. I knelt, my head spinning, as I continued to heave, tears streaming down my face.

Severin and Henri burst in from the other room.

Henri laughed. "You had a party and didn't invite us?"

"What were you thinking?" Severin was aghast as he took in the scene: the bottle of wine, the speckled mess on my shirt and the floor. He wrinkled his nose at the smell and I wobbled, woozy and chagrined.

"Come on," he turned to Henri. "Help me get him cleaned up before Mama comes home."

They got me into new clothes, rinsed out my old ones and cleaned the floor, cursing at the stench as they went. By the time Mama got home, I was resting in bed and they'd stitched together a story. I'd grown queasy after coming in from running around, vomiting while she was out. Perhaps I was getting a flu. Perhaps it was something I ate.

11

WINTER 1941 – MONSIEUR ADLER AT DRANCY

As the winter of 1941 arrived, conditions in Drancy worsened. Due to the unfinished state of the buildings, there was a several-inch gap between the windows and the walls, which caused a draft. The gaps had provided fresh air in the summer, but as the temperature dropped the rooms were constantly cold. There was no access to medical care for the internees, so those who fell ill usually grew sicker. We didn't know it at the time, but my father was among those who fell ill. Monsieur Adler, our upstairs neighbor, also got sick, developing appendicitis. He had lived above us for as long as I could remember and, years earlier, when I was only five years old, he'd shown me a real kindness.

In the fall of 1938, Aunt Maryla and her husband, Uncle Romek, visited us from Brussels. She had been the first to pack a suitcase and flee Warsaw for a brighter future. Her husband was a successful businessman; he manufactured scarves and ties in his small sewing factory and sold them from the building's storefront. Uncle Romek carried himself with the straight-backed air of a man who has left physical labor behind, one who can now safely wear jewelry on his soft clean, hands. He and Aunt Maryla lived with their two children – a boy named Severin like my brother who was eight, and a girl, Micheline, who was five – in an Art Deco townhouse in Brussels, and they came to Paris frequently. Every time they visited they brought colorful silk gifts: This time my mother got a scarf covered in swollen blue paisley raindrops; my brothers and I received matching plaid ties. It was always nice to get a gift, but I couldn't help but wish that Uncle Romek owned a toy store.

On a crisp Saturday night, with the sounds of the city floating through the window, Papa straightened his new tie while Mama applied lipstick. They were getting ready to join the crowds below and head out to a Jewish nightclub with our aunt and uncle, and we were to be left home alone.

"We'll be home before midnight and you can each have a cookie with your tea," Mama said. "Sevek, you are in charge." She kissed each of us, her lipstick leaving a stamp on our cheek.

With my parents gone, we could turn up the radio as loud as we wanted. At night, my brothers and I listened to Radio Paris, often long after my parents had gone to bed. Mama and Papa slept on the other side of the wall, directly opposite the radio. If we were too loud, Papa pounded the plywood until we turned the dial down, forcing us to lean in close to hear our stories. When we heard our father turning over in bed – the groan of the wooden platform, the sigh of the mattress – we knew we could go back to listening and laughing again. When we heard the rumble of his snores, the dial went up another notch.

The kettle whistled and Henri got up to pour the tea. The steam rose in ribbons from our cups. I raised my cup to my lips and was surprised to find it hot to the touch. Startled, I dropped the cup and the hot tea poured down the front of my pajamas, scalding me through my clothes. There was the briefest delay, a moment of confusion, before the pain slammed into me knifelike. The cup shattered on the floor and I screamed.

Severin leapt from his chair and ran over to me. He pulled the wet pajamas off me, exposing my belly and the red, raw skin.

"It's okay, it's okay. Calm down," Severin said. He tried to get me to quiet down, but I couldn't. The pain seared and consumed everything. It was white and hot and red and loud. It ripped through me and surrounded me and there was nothing else in the world but that pain. I screamed and screamed.

There was a loud knock at the door and Henri ran to open it. Our upstairs neighbor, Monsieur Adler, rushed into the apartment, his shirt untucked and his face frantic with worry. "Is someone hurt? Where are your parents? What happened?" The questions tumbled out of him as he looked around the apartment.

"Bernard's burned himself – he spilled tea and now his stomach is red. I think it's bad. We can't get him to stop crying." Henri pointed to the angry patch on my stomach and Monsieur Adler sucked air in quickly, clearly surprised at the burn. I continued to wail.

"Our parents are out at a nightclub," Severin said. "Henri, turn the radio off! They aren't going to be home for another hour at least." Severin was desperate to hand over the reins to an adult. This was more than he had bargained for tonight.

Monsieur Adler went to the sink, took one of my mother's washcloths, and ran cool water over it. He came back and sat next to me.

"Shhh, shhh, it's going to be okay," he soothed. I couldn't stop shaking. Monsieur Adler held the cool cloth to my belly with one hand and wrapped his other arm around me. I'd never been this close to our quiet neighbor: We didn't know him well. He lived alone with no wife or children and had never socialized with my parents.

"There, there, you're doing very well Bernard," Monsieur Adler smiled at me. "Very brave."

He turned to my brothers. "I'll stay until your parents get home. Bernard is going to be fine." Monsieur Adler lifted the cloth and peeked under it. The blisters were already forming, bubbling up from my stomach.

"Are you sure?" Henri asked, looking terrified. "It sounds like he's going to die."

I looked at our neighbor. Was I going to die? It felt like I *could* die, the pain was so fierce.

Monsieur Adler patted my leg reassuringly. "I'm quite sure. He'll be fine, but he's going to have a very bad burn."

He sat with me for over an hour. Gradually, more from exhaustion than from relief, my sobs subsided into a muffled whimper. My body shuddered in that way it does after a hard cry. I snuffled and leaned into Monsieur Adler. His striped shirt was frayed at the edges and what had originally been white was now a drab gray. I could tell that it was not laundered with the same care that my mother put into our clothes. Monsieur Adler had no one to wash his shirts, and I wondered briefly if that made him sad. I would not like to live alone, I thought. He smelled vaguely of herbs, of one of the little green leafy plants that we walked by regularly at the Marché d'Aligre, plants that Mama didn't use in her cooking but that he apparently did. His arm was still around me and he looked down and smiled again; his glasses were smudged and his breath had the sweet, stale smell of the wine he'd had with dinner.

When we heard our parents coming up the stairs Henri ran out to the landing and shouted down. My parents were very surprised to see our upstairs neighbor in the apartment, sitting quietly with his arm around me. They conferred with Monsieur Adler briefly in Yiddish, thanking him for his kindness before whisking me out of the apartment to the nearby Saint-Antoine hospital – the same hospital where I'd been born.

Once there we were ushered down the well-lit hallway, my mother's evening shoes clicking on the linoleum, the smell of disinfectant in the air. A nurse bandaged my abdomen and gave me something bitter to swallow. Soon the edges of my world were soft and cloud-like; Papa lifted me and I burrowed into him, inhaling his familiar, comforting smell as he set out toward home. I drifted to sleep with my head on his shoulder, my legs swinging with each step he took, and woke the next day confident that I would indeed live through my ordeal, although the burn continued to sting for several weeks.

We went back to smiling and greeting Monsieur Adler when we passed him in the stairway, but it was different somehow, more personal, less perfunctory. "How's that wound healing?" he asked me the first time we passed on the stairs, and I lifted my shirt to show him the bandage. Monsieur Adler looked the same when he came into the courtyard with his groceries, the baguette peeking out from behind the foliage of his herbs and vegetables, wearing his slightly shabby shirts. Yet I felt a new connection to him, the way you do when you've shared a harrowing experience with someone.

The blisters gradually healed and the splatter mark settled into a rough-edged scar that remained visible for many years. I could trace the outline with my finger, the territory of my burn.

———

There was no doctor at Drancy, at least in those early months. When Monsieur Adler came down with appendicitis, there was nothing for him to do but hold his stomach and pray that it got better. But appendicitis doesn't get better without medical care. Instead, the pain grew until he lay coiled on the floor of his barracks, arms wrapped around himself to tamp down the misery. Untreated, the appendix burst and the poison spread throughout his blood. He shuddered with fever and rocked with pain until, finally, he died on the cold stone floor, gripping his belly, his face pressed into the soiled straw.

My father heard his screams from a neighboring room. I don't know how he recognized Monsieur Adler's wail. Does something from the timbre of a man's speaking voice remain, even when he is reduced to his most basic animal self, even when he is beyond speech and howling in pain? Papa could not leave his block to get to Monsieur Adler, but I hope that someone was with him. I hope that someone held his hand and whispered soothing words in his ear. I hope that he was not alone when he died.

12

NOVEMBER 1941 – THE DRANCY
EIGHT HUNDRED

Monsieur Adler was one of dozens who died in those first months, neglected in the appalling conditions of the barracks. Finally, in November, Jean Tisne, the doctor of the Prefecture of Police, alerted a commission of German doctors who, taking advantage of an opportunity created by Dannecker's brief absence from the camp, decided to liberate those who were the sickest, about 800 men. First, a number of frail internees with surnames starting with the letters A to the letter K were freed. The next day another 150, from L to Z, were sent home. My father, malnourished and very ill, was one of those 150 selected to be released. On the morning of November 4, 1941, Papa stumbled, ghostlike, out of the gates of Drancy. At 11 a.m. shortly after he departed, a telephone call halted further releases.

Papa called from a café near the camp and reached Madame Raymond, who managed the single shared phone line for the residents of 5 rue de Charonne. She shouted up to my mother, who raced downstairs to the Raymonds' apartment to talk to him. As soon as Mama hung up, she called the family doctor, who came to our apartment and waited, his hands clasped primly on the black doctor's bag in his lap, his owlish eyes staring ahead through his spectacles.

"Let's wait downstairs in the courtyard," I said, eager to see Papa the minute he came home.

"It's too cold outside, Binem," Mama said firmly but sympathetically, "and it's going to take a while for your father to get here – Drancy is an hour away by train." But she couldn't hide her nerves as she stood at the courtyard window, tapping the sill and looking down, standing so close that she fogged the glass with her breath.

"I should make something to eat," she said suddenly. "He's probably going to be hungry for a home-cooked meal." She nodded to herself, moved away from the window, and started preparing a meatloaf sandwich. My brothers and I moved to the window, so now there were three sets of mouths breathing hot air on the cold glass, fogging it.

After almost an hour, my mother stood up from her dining chair. "I'm going to go downstairs now and wait with Madame Raymond," she said. I stood to follow – we all did – but she held up her hand. "Your father is going to want to see all of you, of course, but he'll probably be very tired. I don't want to overwhelm him. I'll go downstairs to meet him, and you boys will wait here. With Dr. Weinberger."

I must have looked disappointed because she added, "Binem, I know it's hard to wait. We've already waited so long. But this is for the best."

"Your mother's right," Dr. Weinberger added. "Your father is very tired and, from what he told your mother, he's also quite ill. It's best not to overwhelm him."

Finally, we heard the sounds of shuffling up the stairs, a far wearier version of what we were used to, and we threw open the door. Nothing could have prepared us for the shock of his appearance. I gasped. He was so gaunt and pale that I wondered how he'd climbed the stairs at all. His coat hung from his shoulders like from a wire hanger. His cheeks were hollow and waxy, his movements stooped and slow. His eyes, enormous in his wizened face, were glassy and dull. His normally smooth face was covered in a rough beard, and his hair was tangled and matted. His state of dishevelment made it seem as if he'd been gone for years rather than months. He was so unrecognizable that I quickly looked down at his right hand, scanning for his stump of an index finger. I needed to make sure that it was not an interloper, someone claiming to be my father.

Mama was at his side, propping him up. She escorted him to their bedroom while we all stood back and watched. She got him to the bed and then came back out, and Dr. Weinberger went in and examined Papa thoroughly. We sat at the table, unable to speak. When the doctor emerged from the bedroom, he spoke quietly to my mother in Yiddish.

"It's very lucky that he was released," the doctor said. "He would not have been able to endure much more. He will be fine, but he is extremely ill and you need to follow my instructions very carefully." He scribbled on a piece of paper as he spoke. "For the first five days, he must drink only broth. He must not have any food. Perhaps he may have a bit of bread after the first couple of days."

He paused to reread his instructions before handing them to her "This is very important," he added. "He *must* not eat very much initially, and certainly not any rich foods. It might seem like what he needs, but it would make him worse, could even kill him – cause a heart attack perhaps."

We were lucky that our doctor was aware of the risks. Although it was not well understood at the time, refeeding syndrome would become all too familiar at the end of the war when well-intentioned soldiers fed starving camp survivors foods like chocolate upon their rescue. Their emaciated bodies were ill-prepared for such rich foods, and many of those who survived the horrors of the camp died of cardiac arrest in the days after their release.

Mama ran a washcloth over Papa's skeletal limbs, cleaning the sores and insect bites. She washed him as if he were a child, or a thing that might break. His clothes, filthy and smelling of sickness, lay moldering on the floor until she was done cleaning him, and then she threw them away.

In the days that followed, she sat by his bed and watched over him, and sometimes I stood at the door and watched, too. Mostly, he slept. But occasionally he stirred, his eyes opened, and she would put a cup of broth to his mouth. Finally, he woke and smiled at her with parched lips.

"Don't worry, Rikla, you can't get rid of me that easily," he croaked.

"Oh, Yosel," Mama said. She put her head in her hands and the tears poured down her cheeks.

My father was among the very first Jewish internees at the Drancy camp, one of the camp's "founders." A total of 70,000 would pass through during World War II. Before the official liberation of the camp, only 800 of those 70,000 – the 800 who were released in November 1941 during Dannecker's two-day absence – got out. Most internees were sent to Auschwitz, where nearly all of them died. My father, a Polish laborer who could speak only rudimentary French and had neither money nor connections, was among the 1% who returned home.

Papa stayed in bed for a week or so, gradually regaining color and strength. His cheeks filled in slowly until he began to look like the man I remembered. By the beginning of 1942, he'd regained much of his weight and was back at work making furniture. Business picked up again: Papa learned that wealthy Germans enjoyed collecting fine French furniture as much as wealthy Parisians did. Henri was apprenticing with my father again, learning to varnish in the French style, while Severin resumed training as an upholsterer under Monsieur Tsibulsky. I was in grammar school, in the *cours élémentaire* 2 level. It seemed like we'd survived the worst and our lives returned to a normal, predictable schedule. As long as we adhered to all the restrictions, we thought we would be okay.

Around us, the war continued. The United States declared war on Japan in December 1941 after the Japanese bombed Pearl Harbor, a US naval base in Hawaii. In a move that baffled many, Hitler then declared war on the United States. President Roosevelt, initially reluctant to join the fray of what was until then a European war, had no choice but to declare war in response. The war was now officially worldwide.

Meanwhile, the Nazis were moving forward with their plans for the Jews. On January 20, 1942, 15 senior Nazi officials gathered in the Berlin suburb of Wannsee for a top-secret meeting. Over lunch, in a mansion on the edge of a snow-covered lake, they discussed the details of the Final Solution, the plan whereby most of the Jews of German-occupied Europe would be deported to concentration camps in Poland and murdered. Reinhard Heydrich, chief of Reich Security and, at six feet, three inches the tallest man in the room, led the conference, designed to ensure the cooperation of all officials involved. Heydrich was the primary architect behind Kristallnacht, and Hitler referred to him as "the man with the iron heart."

Hitler had announced the Final Solution in 1941, but the precise plan – the actual logistics – had not yet been determined. Mobile gassing units had been used for months, but over lunch that day in January, Heydrich announced a plan to install large, permanent facilities in the new camp of Auschwitz. The officials met for less than two hours, and not a single man objected to the proposed plan.

A couple of months later, on March 27, 1942, the first transport left from Drancy for Auschwitz, carrying 1,112 deportees. On June 22, another 1,000 left Drancy for Auschwitz. A thousand more departed in July. And so it continued.

Drancy release papers for Joseph Parkiet
4, November 1941

13

STARS AND MARBLES

On May 29, 1942, a new pronouncement was issued: Jews in France were ordered to wear the six-pointed star that they were already wearing in Germany and Poland. Anyone older than six had to wear it.

In a cruel twist, textile ration tickets had to be used to buy the yellow cloth star. Like food, our clothing consumption was rationed, with each article of clothing having a unique ticket value. Mama already was mending our clothes until they were beyond repair, so it was infuriating to have to use our limited textile allowance on something thrust upon us. Failure to wear the star was punishable by fine, imprisonment, or even death. We wore the star.

This treatment was not new for the Jewish people. As far back as the 13th century, Jews of Europe were required by law to wear badges or other distinguishing garments such as pointed hats. The practice continued throughout the Middle Ages and the Renaissance but was largely phased out during the 17th and 18th centuries. With the French Revolution and the emancipation of Jews throughout the 19th century, the wearing of Jewish badges was abolished throughout Western Europe. It was back now.

My mother sat at our table, sewing one of the yellow cotton stars onto my father's suit jacket. Across the German-occupied areas of Europe, Jews wore a variety of such stars. Ours bore the word Juif written in a mock Hebraic font. Papa watched her as she worked, a cigarette dangling from his mouth, his fingers beating out a slow tap-tap on the table.

"You know," Papa said, "it's about time we had a formal family photo taken. We don't have a single one."

My mother looked up from her sewing, clearly surprised. She rested her hands in her lap and stared at him, trying to determine if he was serious.

"Yosel, you want to have a photo taken now, just after I've sewed this star onto all of our clothing?" she asked.

"Why not?" he responded. He'd clearly anticipated her reaction. "I'm proud of you, of our beautiful family. Why not now?"

My father, the provocateur. He knew, of course, that wearing the star was intended to invoke shame. But though he was still weakened from Drancy, though his clavicle still poked through his undershirt, he was determined to wear the star with pride.

On June 6, a Saturday, we got dressed in our best suits to take a formal family photo. "Did you notice, Binem, that Roy Rogers' sheriff's badge in *Sheriff of Tombstone* is a Star of David?" Papa asked as he straightened my tie. My father and I used to go to the movies almost every Wednesday, just the two of us. We loved traditional Westerns, popular at the time, and our favorites starred Gary Cooper and John Wayne. We weren't really Roy Rogers fans – singing cowboys weren't our style – but he would do in a pinch.

"Really?"

"Yes. Also James Stewart in *Destry Rides Again*. A lot of the sheriff's badges are the six-pointed star. Just like the Jewish star."

"Destry wasn't a sheriff, he was a deputy," I pointed out.

"That's true." My father agreed. "But he wore the star. And so do you. And so do I. And where does a sheriff wear his star?"

I looked down at my chest and the star on the left side of my body.

"On the left. Just like us."

"That's right. So I'll be the sheriff, and you can be my deputy. What do you think about that, Goldener Kop?"

I thought that sounded fine. We walked as a family – a sheriff and his deputies with the stars emblazoned on our chests – down rue du Faubourg Saint Antoine to a small neighborhood photography studio. A bald man with a vacant expression and a face like an empty dinner plate, white and round, had us pose in front of a pale backdrop, our dark clothes putting us in sharp relief. What must he have been thinking, this man so used to commemorating birthdays, weddings, and other celebrations? I can only imagine. Whatever it was, he didn't share it. Mama, Henri, Severin, and Papa stood in a line, shortest to tallest, with me standing in front of Papa in my short pants suit, my white ankle socks peeking out from my black shoes. In the picture, we are all gazing slightly off to our right at some unseen object. Now this photo hangs in the Shoah Memorial in Paris.

On Monday I returned to school, a star sewn onto my uniform. A few other boys in my class wore the same star. Madame Roche started the day as she always did, with us sitting at our desks, our hands clasped in front of us. She stood at the front of the class, ramrod straight, chin in the air, and asserted herself authoritatively.

"You have probably noticed that some of your classmates are wearing yellow stars on their uniforms," she said.

She paused, giving everyone time to look around. There was a shifting of chairs, a gentle rustling as we all looked around.

"Their clothing might be slightly different now, but they themselves are not," she said. "I want to make it clear, very clear, that I will not tolerate any disrespect."

She looked at each boy sitting at his desk; she made eye contact with all of us individually as if by staring into our eyes she could instill her admonition into our very souls. Maybe it was my imagination, but it seemed that her eyes softened when she met mine, that the edges of her mouth turned up in the subtlest of smiles.

"They are the same boys that you have always known. They are your friends, and you will treat them as such," she finished with a nod, and she turned back to the chalkboard and began to write a math problem in her neat, sideways script.

Maybe it was because of what she said, maybe not, but none of my classmates even seemed to notice the star after that. Or maybe it was because I wore it like a sheriff's badge, a star not of cotton but hard, shiny brass.

The courtyard of my school was perfect for playing marbles. Unlike the cobblestone courtyard of 5 rue de Charonne, École Keller's courtyard was smooth concrete. During *récréation*, my schoolmates and I would draw wobbly chalk lines to indicate the shooting line and crouch down, our faces pressed to the ground, squinting as we aimed. When we played, we played for keeps: If we won, we claimed the loser's marble as our own. The pockets of our school smocks were filled with clay marbles that, mottled and multicolored, looked like little planets that might contain life.

When the bell rang, Madame Vidal called out to everyone. "Boys, form a line right here in front of me," she said, waving us over. "Quickly, quickly." We stood, red circles on our bare knees marking where they had been pressed into the concrete. We lined up single file, so close that the hot breath of the boy behind me tickled my ear.

We did this each day after récréation, our mouths open, tongues out to

66

receive bitter vitamin pills. Food was scarce and we were not getting the amount our growing bodies needed: The vitamins were intended to help get us additional nutrients. As we waited for our pills, we fidgeted, feet shuffling and scuffing the ground. We stuck our tongues out at each other when our teachers weren't looking, or we pretended to retch and vomit. They put the pills directly in our mouths to make sure we actually took them, then handed us a cup of lukewarm milk to wash the vitamin down.

"Bernard," she said crisply, and I opened my mouth obligingly. She placed the pink pill on my tongue, and the tartness spread immediately. Madame Vidal leaned close to verify that I'd swallowed, her breath smelling of onions. I stood with my chin up, staring directly ahead at nothing, trying not to wrinkle my nose. Another teacher came behind with a glass of milk, which I gulped down. The boy behind me made wet choking sounds as if he might actually throw up, and I inched forward in case he did.

France had initiated food rationing before the German invasion, in September 1940, following guidelines similar to those implemented throughout Europe. Under the system, adults were granted a miserly 300 grams of meat per week, the size of three decks of cards. Cheese was also part of the weekly food rationing, doled out with a similarly meager allocation: Adults were permitted 50 grams per week, about equal to half a stick of butter. Butter, the much-needed fat in a hardworking adult's diet, was also rationed. So was bread. Fruit and vegetables were not rationed but were scant, particularly in cities such as Paris, because under occupied France, almost all of the farmed produce that would normally have been sent to Paris was diverted to supply the German army. People in the country fared better because they could grow their own fruit and vegetables. As the war went on, root vegetables like turnips, rutabaga, and the oft-maligned Jerusalem artichoke became staples of the Parisian diet. Chocolate was unattainable, so my beloved pain au chocolat was a thing of the past. The average person consumed about 950 calories each day, about half of what they should get. The entire city of Paris was slowly starving.

The burden of managing our family's meals fell to my mother, who had experienced rationing as a child in Poland but never expected to endure it in France. Now, like everyone else in Paris, she stood in long lines cradling her wicker basket, waiting to get what she could. My mother spoke only basic French and, while she'd learned how to navigate the markets, she still depended greatly on Severin for translation. He helped her sort through her ration booklet, removing the different colored tickets with care. Tickets needed to be managed judiciously to last until the next booklet was issued. But having a ticket didn't guarantee that you could find food: Many got to the front of the line only to find everything gone. Here the courtyard helped again, whether it was Monsieur Meyer stowing away a bit of *jambon* [ham] *de Bayonne* or, next door, Madame Reginaud reserving some milk at her épicerie.

Other less fortunate Parisians – both Jews and non-Jews alike – had to turn to more dangerous ways to survive. In response to rationing and the scarcity of food, instances of the *marché noir* [black market] sprung up around Paris like mushrooms, feeding on the decay of the city. The marché noir thrived throughout the rest of the country as well, including the southern part now known as the Free Zone of Vichy France. Uncle Israel, no longer able to make a living sewing garments when textiles were strictly rationed, began dealing cigarettes in Lyon. He and Aunt Sabine had fled Paris during the initial exodus with their two daughters Micheline and Huguette. After the Germans claimed the northern half of France, they banned all evacuated Jews from returning to Paris, so my aunt and uncle opted to remain in Lyon, relinquishing the polished floors and stylish decor of their beloved apartment to the Germans. With few options available, Uncle Israel must have thought that dealing in the black market was worth the risk. He would turn out to be very wrong.

Parkiet family portrait, June 1942. Left to right: Rikla, Henri, Severin, Joseph. I am standing in front, between Severin and my father.

14

JULY 15–16, 1942 – THE GREAT ROUNDUP

Black Thursday. In America, those two words refer to the stock market crash on October 24, 1929. In Germany, *Schwarzer Donnerstag* refers to August 15, 1940, when the German Luftwaffe suffered its heaviest losses during the WWII Battle of Britain. For the French, *jeudi noir* refers to the July 16, 1942, roundup of over 12,000 Jews. It's also known as The Great Roundup and the Vel'd'Hiv Roundup. By any name, it was a bleak day in French history.

The day before, July 15, began like any other day that summer. In past years, Paris would have been recovering from the festivities of Bastille Day, but Germans forbade the celebration of le 14 Juillet in occupied France. Before the sun had crested over the buildings lining rue de Charonne, Severin went down the street to Monsieur Tsibulsky's workshop, climbing a flight of creaky stairs to begin work in the cramped atelier. Henri and Papa crossed the courtyard to sand down an armoire they'd received a few days before, and Mama and I went to the Marché d'Aligre. Around 1 p.m. everyone came home for lunch, and we sat down to meatloaf, mashed potatoes, and beets. An hour later, there was a series of quick, hard knocks on our door. Papa got up to open it and Madame Nicolas rushed into the apartment. This in itself was odd, as she had never entered our home before, and was usually at work at that time.

"Excuse me, Monsieur Parkiet, Madame Parkiet," Madame Nicolas said. She did not speak Yiddish, so she spoke to my parents in simple French. "This is very important. You must leave!" She waved her arm toward the door quickly as though she was sweeping us out of the apartment. "Police are coming. Tomorrow morning. Go now. Do not stay here in the morning! You will be arrested."

She turned toward my father. "Like Drancy," she added, knowing that this would make the point, if nothing else would.

"Please. Leave. Soon." The fact that she used only a few words made them all the more urgent.

"You understand?" she asked.

My father paled. I suppose that in the several seconds of silence that followed he was imagining his family in that camp. Our round faces gone gaunt. Our bodies frail and withering beneath lice-infested clothing. He had barely survived, and I'm sure he knew that we would not. "Yes," he said quietly. "When?"

"Tomorrow morning, very early. I saw today at Préfecture de Police. A list. All Parkiet names on it. Métro will close. Do not use Métro. Police will be there." She finished and looked down at the floor. Her cheeks were still flushed from rushing from work. The Préfecture de Police was on the Île de la Cité, near Notre Dame, easily a 30-minute walk from our apartment.

My parents whispered in the corner while Madame Nicolas stood there. Her blue eyes were rimmed with tears and she seemed unwilling to leave until she had extracted a promise that we were going to vacate our apartment.

"You saw *all* our names, Madame? Even Binem and Rikla?" The idea that women and small children were going to be arrested seemed almost impossible to believe.

"Yes, Monsieur Parkiet, everyone." With a sweep of her hand, she gestured at all of us to ensure she was understood. "Many families, many mothers, many children will be arrested."

Kind Madame Nicolas. Brave Madame Nicolas. Our upstairs neighbor, the one who used to help my pregnant mother carry groceries upstairs, was helping us again. With the simple action of slipping out of her office at the police station to warn us, she risked her life. Only a lucky few received such warnings. What she did was illegal in the eyes of the Vichy regime, and if she'd been caught she almost certainly would have been killed: yanked from her home and dragged down the street, her black dress flailing behind her, to be lined up against a wall with other "traitors." A member of the police – maybe even someone with whom she worked every day – would have shot a bullet into her brain.

After she finished speaking, the air in the apartment felt heavy. It was as though her words had sucked the oxygen from the room. No one moved as my father stood, his hand on his brow, as if trying to pull a solution through his fingertips. Outside, I heard the clip of horse hooves on the cobblestones, the grunts of men lifting furniture from a carriage. The world was proceeding as though nothing had changed, but inside our apartment, time had stopped. A harsh clang – the sound of a fork hitting the floor – made everyone jump. Severin bent and placed it back on his plate, cheeks flushed.

The sound seemed to shake Papa from his trance. He turned back to Madame Nicolas, and both of my parents moved toward her.

"Thank you, Madame Nicolas," he said. Mama took her hands, cradled them, and said, "We are very grateful."

"Yes. Well, I'm sorry. So sorry." She looked at all of us boys, her eyes red-rimmed, tears pooling. "So very sorry. I must get back to work. Be careful."

Papa turned to Mama. "Pack up whatever food we have."

He pivoted to look at me and my brothers. He lit a Gauloise and inhaled deeply, staring at the three of us.

"We will go to my workshop. Bring the gas masks, nothing else. We must leave the apartment looking exactly as it always is or it will look suspicious. I'll be right back."

"Eat, eat," my mother said, urging us to finish our supper even though she had moved away from her own plate and was packing up food.

"I'm not hungry, Mama. Let me help you instead," Severin said and stood up.

"No, eat your supper."

I realize now that she had no idea when we would next have a real meal.

By the time Papa returned, food was packed and we were sitting at the table, ready to go. I hadn't finished my meal, but, like my brothers, I was no longer hungry.

We crossed the courtyard to Stairway 9 with my father leading the way, the rest of us following silently behind in a state of shock. We followed him straight into his workshop, with the familiar jars of varnish and alcohol cluttering his table; he'd only been home for the midday meal, so his work for the day was not yet complete. He locked the door. For a moment he looked as if he might make a half-hearted attempt to continue working, but then he stopped, cleaned up his supplies, and put them away. He stared out the window. My mother swept the floor and we pushed the furniture to the corners of the room so we could sit together in the center. We had nothing with us. I didn't know what to do, and I was afraid to ask questions. Eventually, we lay down on the floor and tried to sleep, the cool seeping up through the stone and into our bodies. I curled up next to my mother, my head resting in the cove between her ribs and arm.

I woke up several times during the night, and I could tell that my father was at the window, though I could not see him because the moon was new and the sky was as black as spilled ink. I could smell his cigarette and see the glowing tip, the flare of the ember when he inhaled. One time, I rolled over and looked at Severin and saw he was also awake, lying on his back, his chest rising and falling slowly, his eyes small and naked without his glasses. Sometimes Papa would stand, sometimes he would sit. It was not until almost daybreak that his silhouette became visible in the window against the melancholy sky.

At dawn, workers began to enter the courtyard, moving furniture and exchanging small talk. The Italian painter, a genial man who sang opera while he worked outside, set up his horsehair brushes and began mixing his colors as the sun climbed in the sky. The Italian resembled a paintbrush himself: He was thin and paint-speckled, with a dark bristle of hair that sprouted from his head. Soon the familiar sounds of Puccini and Verdi, sung in his robust tenor, bounced off the courtyard walls. For most of Paris, it was just another Thursday. But not for us, and we stayed in the workshop. We emptied our bladders into the chamber pot and nibbled at the food that Mama had brought, our stomachs queasy and hollow. With nothing to drink, our mouths were dry and the day-old bread stuck in our throats. Father continued to stare out of the window, smoking.

Throughout the city, Jews were being arrested. Starting in the darkness of early morning, 4,500 French police had deployed in small teams to scour the city. They apprehended over 13,000 Jews, most of them women and children because many men had already been arrested. Some argued, waving their papers, confident that logic could save them. Surely there had been a mistake. (There hadn't.) Some acquiesced quietly, thinking their politeness would help them. (It wouldn't.) Some, brave or foolish, ran. Most who ran were shot, but a few lucky ones got away (for now).

Those arrested were taken to a nearby gym or school, just as Papa had been taken to the Japy gymnasium the previous August. From there, single adults and families with older children were sent to Drancy. Families with children under 16, like ours, were taken to the Vélodrome d'Hiver, the immense glass-covered sports stadium in the 15th arrondissement. Upon arrival, with the sounds of shouting and wailing all around them, the bewildered and frightened families were directed to a corner where they could grab a bag and stuff it with straw to make a mattress.

Only foreign-born Jews were arrested that day, almost all from Eastern Europe. In the two years since Germany had taken Paris, attitudes toward immigrants had worsened considerably. The anti-immigrant stance was a significant departure from what Aunt Sabine had described when she urged my father to join her in Paris; it was also different from what my father experienced when he arrived in 1931, sure that he'd finally escaped the oppressive antisemitism of Poland.

Before World War I, Jewish immigrants had entered France gradually and in small numbers. When they arrived, they quietly made themselves a part of the French fabric, learning the language, adopting the secular and nationalistic ways that are uniquely French. Directly after the war, France opened its doors to foreigners to replenish its depleted workforce. Six million French died during the Great War, so the country needed people to work in its fields and factories. During this golden period of immigration, it was as though Lady Liberty herself had stepped out of Delacroix's famous painting to lead a new generation of immigrants to a better life in the French Republic. But these immigrants were different from those who had preceded them. When Aunt Sabine and Uncle Israel and my parents arrived, they were part of a large wave of immigrants from Poland who congregated in a small cluster of neighborhoods where other friends and family had recently settled, forming large groups that remained socially and economically isolated from the rest of French society. The religious Jews moved to the 3rd and 4th arrondissements. The more secular, like us, settled around rue du Faubourg St. Antoine, Belleville, and Montmartre.

My parents loved their chosen home of Paris, but they were slow to adapt to the French way of life. Both had difficulty learning the language, although Father picked it up faster because of his daily exposure to clients. Since all of their friends were from Poland and they always spoke Yiddish when gathered in each other's apartments for meals and holidays, their inability to speak French didn't seem much of a problem. But while it must have been a great comfort to have others who shared their culture and language, it was also a barrier that prevented full assimilation. As much as my parents loved France, they were never French.

This separateness was one of the reasons that Jews were the primary target of the renewed xenophobia. When production plummeted in the 1930s and the job market shrank, the French looked with increasing suspicion at foreign workers who they now felt were taking the few jobs still available. While the majority of immigrants in France were from Italy and Spain, it was the Polish Jews who engendered the most resentment. Many French citizens, including even the French Jews, found the Polish immigrants coarse and uncouth. Now we were easy targets.

Late Thursday morning, Madame Raymond walked past the window of my father's workshop, looked up, and gave a tight-lipped smile: The gendarmes had come and gone. Later, she came to see us, bringing fresh bread and a pitcher of water.

"I don't think it's safe for you to stay here much longer. It will not take long for the gendarmes to realize that you have a workshop here and to think to come here to look for you."

The lease was in my father's name, a fact that would not be hard to discover.

"Yes, Madame Raymond, you are right." My father paced the narrow space as he spoke, thinking aloud. "I have an idea."

I don't know how he made the arrangements, but two days later there was a plan. We would move to an underutilized warehouse on the fourth floor of Stairway 6. The unit was leased to Monsieur Thibou, a Catholic cabinetmaker who was one of my father's clients. His main workshop was off Stairway 5, but he also leased an adjoining warehouse, accessible from Stairway 6. Monsieur Thibou agreed to empty his warehouse and let us move in until everything settled down. That would prove to be much longer than anyone anticipated.

15

JULY 18, 1942 – STAIRWAY 6

We half shuffled, half stumbled into the warehouse, weary, scared, and disoriented from three nights of sleeping on the workshop floor. The room – a rectangle with two small windows running along its length and a door at either end – was almost empty. The plaster walls were peeling and a seemingly random assortment of furniture was scattered around as if abandoned. An unfinished armoire occupied the far end near the door to Monsieur Thibou's shop. On the wall opposite the windows was a black potbelly stove with a pile of wood stacked next to it. A large box made from a poplar tree sat to the side of the stove. Next to it was a wooden chair with a wicker seat.

Monsieur Thibou followed us in from Stairway 6, removing his hat as he entered and holding it against his chest. Freed from the hat, a curl of black hair fell across his long, narrow face. Tall and slender, Monsieur Thibou moved lightly, with an almost feline elegance. He looked about my father's age and was easily half a foot taller than him with high cheekbones and thick, wavy hair. I'd seen Monsieur Thibou many times before, but always in my father's workshop – he was one of Papa's most dedicated clients and frequently stopped by to see how a particular piece was progressing. Unfailingly polite, he'd knock at the door gently before peeking inside. "Am I interrupting anything?" he always asked, with an apologetic half-smile on his face, and my father would greet Monsieur Thibou's mildness with his typical boldness, smiling widely and waving him inside, eager to show off his work.

"I realize that this room is not much, and I'm sorry that I cannot do better," Monsieur Thibou said, sweeping back his forelock and looking around the dusty space as if assessing it for the first time and finding it wanting. "I hope you will be comfortable enough here. We will bring you wood for the stove when you need it. But you can only use the stove during the day when everyone is here and working." My mother walked over to the wicker chair and lowered herself into it wearily with a small sigh.

No one lived in this part of the building, so it was inhabited only during the day. "If there is activity at night – if smoke is seen coming from the chimney, or if light is visible in the window – you will raise suspicion," Monsieur Thibou said. "And that," he finished, tapping his hat against his leg, "will not be good for any of us." We all nodded. My mother combed down the pieces of unraveling rattan that popped up from the wicker chair like cowlicks. She would repair that.

A pair of tradesmen carried in a workbench, entering from the interior door that connected the two ateliers. Through the open door, I could see the other room, the sawdust-covered floor, an unfinished walnut sideboard peeking out from under a varnish-stained tarp. Monsieur Grósz, who was Monsieur Thibou's business partner, glanced up from his ledger, a pencil in his hand, and appraised us through the doorway before frowning slightly and looking back down. After the workmen positioned the bench by the window and left, Monsieur Thibou walked over to it, the wooden soles of his shoes echoing in the almost empty room. He ran his palm across the surface of the bench. "I will start bringing you work right away," Monsieur Thibou said. For the foreseeable future, this bench would be Papa's workshop, this room our home.

"Thank you," Papa replied, and the two men shook hands solemnly.

To block easy entry from the shop, my father and Monsieur Thibou pushed the armoire in front of the interior door that connected the two ateliers. "We'll move it to deliver furniture, but otherwise these doors should remain closed," Monsieur Thibou said firmly. "And blocked. Only use that door if absolutely necessary." On the other side, in Monsieur Thibou's workshop, a tall bookshelf was positioned so that the passage was rendered completely invisible to visitors. If we needed to leave the warehouse, we would do so via the doorway to Stairway 6.

"Well," Papa said after Monsieur Thibou had gone back to his atelier, "since this is going to be our home for a while, we should get some things from the apartment."

That evening after dark, Papa, Severin, and Henri slipped back through the courtyard to our apartment. Our front door was marked, the door stile and frame joined together with a wax seal, the color of dried blood, a typical Nazi practice to discourage entry and to make it clear when it had occurred.

Looters were combing the entire arrondissement, taking advantage of the opportunity presented by so many homes left vacant by arrested Jews. Now we burgled our own home, making several trips across the courtyard with pots, clothing, and other essentials. Severin and Henri shouldered over our mattresses, the center swinging between them like the back of an old swayback mare, while Mama and I watched from the warehouse window.

They plopped the two twin mattresses onto the floor next to each other. Mama and Papa would share one mattress, and we would share the other. I nestled in between Henri and Severin with my head at their feet. Normally, Henri would take advantage of the close proximity to pinch or tease me; normally, I would have kicked his face in retaliation with a combination of frustration and delight. But there was nothing normal about any of this and we fell asleep quickly, grateful to have something soft and familiar beneath us.

In the morning, Mama removed all of the stars from our clothing, using a seam ripper to tear out the thread she'd sewn on only weeks before.

A few kilometers away in the 15th arrondissement, families were suffering in the stifling heat of the sealed Vél d'Hiv. The stadium had a glass ceiling that, to protect it from air raids, had been painted a cerulean blue. The tinted glass gave everyone inside a ghoulish aspect. The few functioning bathrooms were locked off because they contained windows that offered the possibility of escape. The stench of urine and excrement quickly became overwhelming, its intensity matched only by the sharp cries of children and their mothers wailing – the pitch of human misery.

Within the space of several days, it seemed the world had been turned upside down. My life was confined to a single room that a grown man could cross in several strides, my view limited to what I could see from two windows. Sometimes I could hear my friends playing ball in the courtyard, their shouts and laughing, but I could not see them. It rained, but I did not splash in puddles in the courtyard in my galoshes; I watched the drops bead like tears on the glass panes. We hid and the Germans searched. They scoured the city, checking papers, knocking on doors, interrogating anyone on the street who provoked their suspicion.

And we prayed that they would not find us.

16

SUMMER 1942 – THE NEW NORMAL

In the first few weeks, with Madame Raymond's support, we went about the more mundane aspects of survival. After she placed a phone call, a young man in suspenders arrived at our door with a black-market ham and some illicitly obtained ration tickets. He hefted the ham in on one shoulder and suspended it from a hook in the ceiling where it swung back and forth whenever my mother shaved off a slice.

Father and Henri worked together in the warehouse, refinishing furniture delivered by Monsieur Thibou's workers. Severin crossed the courtyard to Stairway 9 every morning to work in an upholsterer's atelier, quietly stitching fabric side-by-side with tradesmen who'd watched him roam the courtyard since he was a knobby-kneed boy and who therefore must have known he was hiding there now. "But under no circumstances do you leave the courtyard, Sevek," my father said pointedly. Mama continued to prepare our small meals, repair our worn-out clothing, and generally keep our space tidy. She patched together our life from inside the warehouse, leaving only to empty the chamber pot or get water from the lavatory upstairs. Even I had a job and, according to my father, it was the most important job of all: the daily food shopping.

Before the war, I regularly accompanied my mother on her shopping trips. While we purchased some items from our neighbors, most of our food came from the Marché d'Aligre, a ten-minute walk from home, and we bought meat on one of the many crooked, medieval streets of the Marais from an elderly woman with a squint known as "The Aunt." And, of course, we also regularly visited Madame Reginaud's épicerie, Monsieur Meyer's charcuterie, and, my favorite, Madame Benot's boulangerie.

This prewar shopping was hardly the highlight of my day and, while I enjoyed my mother's company, I went along only because I was too young to be left unattended. Most days I tugged on her hand impatiently or wandered away to explore the scents of other stalls that beckoned, making shopping harder for her.

Now that we were hiding from both French and German authorities, it wasn't safe for my mother to venture to the markets: It wasn't safe for either of my parents to leave the warehouse. What little French they knew was so heavily soaked in a Yiddish accent that a single word would give them away. As the youngest, the smallest, and the one who spoke the most unaccented French, I would raise the least suspicion if seen out and about. However, I wasn't permitted to go as far as the Marché Aligre, which was considered too risky since it would expose me to far more people.

My father pulled out several francs and ration tickets and pressed them into my hand. Then he placed his hands on my shoulders and, bending down, looked at me intently with eyes that were red-rimmed and lined by exhaustion. "Now, what are you going to do?" he asked.

"First, I'll go into Madame Meyer's from the courtyard. I'll go out the front door." This would take me to rue de Charonne but with minimal contact with strangers. "Then I'll go next door to Madame Reginaud's." I lifted the empty blue milk pitcher, which I was to refill. "I'll come straight back, and I'll check to see that I am not followed."

"And what if you think someone is watching you and paying attention to where you are going?"

"I'll go into a different stairway, probably 2 or 4." I needed to avoid Stairway 3 because that's where Titi lived. "If it seems like I'm being followed, I'll climb into the attic and come down Stairway 6 so they don't see me." All of the stairways were connected via a shared attic. If you wanted, you could go into the attic at Stairway 1 and emerge down at the other end of the courtyard at Stairway 7. Having played hide-and-seek in these buildings for years, I was an expert in navigating every nook and cranny. The attic was a particular favorite of mine: Small dormers let light flood in, and the pitch of the roof was tall enough for a child to stand at the ridge point, making it easy for me to run from one end to the other, stirring up many layers of dust as I raced through, the motes flying around like fairies.

"And what will you do if you see any of your friends? If you see Titi?"

I looked down at my worn shoes; the left was untied and the lace curled like a dried worm. Through the open window, I could hear the distant shrieks of other children at play. How badly I wanted to see my friends, particularly Titi. I missed her. Was she worried about me? Did she wonder where I'd gone? We had played together every day, and I'd vanished without a word.

"I won't speak to them, Papa. I will pretend that I don't see them."

"And if Titi calls to you?"

"I won't look. I'll ignore her so she'll think she was mistaken." I felt a stab in my chest even thinking about ignoring Titi. But my father was not to be disobeyed.

"You must, Binem. Tell me you understand how important this is." He looked at me intently, the black holes of his pupils drilling into my own, searching them for weakness.

"I do, Papa." Though of course I didn't, not really. What I did understand was I had to obey him, even though I didn't know why.

He ruffled my head. "Very good, Goldener Kop. You are being very brave."

Even though I needed to avoid my friends, this was a great job! To be able to leave the stuffy air and cramped confines of the warehouse, to be out in our courtyard even if just briefly. To feel the sun's kiss, buttery and soft, on my face! Those daily shopping trips were the only time that I might feel the tickle of a breeze or the pinpricks of rain. So even though I was forbidden to speak with anyone, lest I draw attention to myself, each errand was a burst of freedom. What had once been a dreary chore became my favorite part of the day.

As odd as it may seem, our new life settled into a predictable rhythm. Work was still Monday through Saturday. The francs earned by my father and brothers were folded into my pocket with our purloined ration tickets and I slid them across the counter to purchase food from our neighbors. Maybe because there were often other shoppers present, the transactions were made silently, with never more than a conspiratorial smile. As I strolled back to the warehouse, I swung the refilled pitcher over my head in a circle, making the milk froth like ocean surf, in no hurry to be confined to our room again. Sometimes, Monsieur or Madame Raymond would wink at me as I passed, a welcome acknowledgment that I was still real, that we were not forgotten.

Still, life was far from normal. There were a number of moments that reminded me of this new reality, that reminded me we were hiding from the world.

One afternoon, Father turned from his workbench by the warehouse window, looking ashen. "I just watched all of our belongings being taken out of the apartment," he said. "By gendarmes."

Mama cocked her head to the side as if she wasn't sure she heard right.

"Everything has been taken," he repeated. "I saw our table carried out. All of the chairs. Our bed frame. I don't know ..." He looked down at the floor and paused. He exhaled slowly. "I don't know where they are taking everything, but it's all gone."

We never did find out where they took all of our things, but we never saw them again.

Another day as I watched my mother sew – having little to occupy me, I frequently watched my parents at their work – I noticed that she was making something different, cloth pouches that cinched at the top. What were those? "Mama, what are you making?"

She looked up and managed a wan smile. There were dark half-circles, hammocks of worry, under her eyes. "I am making bags for us in case we need to leave and bring some of our things."

I looked at Henri, bent over a dresser he was sanding. His sleeves were rolled up and a fine wooden dust was sticking to the hairs on his arms, flecking his trousers like a delicate brown snow. He shook his head at me – *Don't ask.* I didn't, but I couldn't help but wonder. If we left, where would we go? Would we go to Drancy, the place that almost killed Papa, the place that returned him to us starving and smelling of death? Maybe Henri was right: Some questions were better left unasked.

I know the answer now. From the Vél d'Hiv stadium, we might have been taken to Drancy, where the conditions had not improved, or we might instead have been bused to either Pithiviers or Beaune-la-Rolande, two camps outside of Paris that were equally overcrowded and filthy. Either way, we would have been together as a family only briefly. Deportations to Auschwitz began in late July, in cattle cars, sealed windowless cars designed for transporting livestock and now used to transport Jews. Children under 14 were initially left behind, so I would have watched helplessly as my family left without me, shoved into railway cars while I stood in the muck and straw with the other young children, many of whom were still in diapers. Some desperate parents thrust their uncomprehending toddlers into the arms of other young children, strangers. Deported without me, my family would have been further separated upon arrival to Auschwitz, or they might have been gassed directly upon arrival to the camp, as so many were.

There's no question that we were extraordinarily lucky to be hiding in a warehouse, with neighbors who kept our secret and cared about us, but I didn't feel lucky at the time. Days were hard, watching from a window as the world went on without us, our lives on pause. Nights were harder. During the workday, while I could not play outside or roam the building, I was at least free to be noisy, to stomp around if I wanted. There was constant vigilance, but there was also normal teasing and squabbling that belied the direness of our circumstances. Papa and Henri chatted as they worked. Smoke puffed out of the chimney from the potbelly stove, and the sour smell of boiled cabbage mingled with the scent of varnish.

During the day, we blended in with the workers around us, the crowds providing anonymity. When the workday was over, men filed out of the courtyard, and Monsieur Raymond locked the cast iron gates. We smothered the fire, and fingers of chill quickly crept in. If the moon was slim and sickle, we lit a single candle, hiding the flame from the window with a homemade screen that surrounded it on three sides so the light could only be seen from a single direction, as if peeking through a barely open door.

Before the war, our evenings were filled with family noise. The radio broadcast the news first, which my parents liked, then tales of adventure that my siblings and I enjoyed. Papa, perpetually surrounded by a cloud of cigarette smoke, regaled us with stories while we played belote. We could also hear the sounds of life in the apartments around us, from the dull thud of steps through the ceiling or the occasional quarreling of Madame and Monsieur Poirier across the hall. Stairway 1 was never completely silent. Even in the middle of the night, when most of Paris was asleep, through the windows facing rue de Charonne you could often hear the irregular, stumbling steps of young people coming home from a night of dancing and drinking, their bursts of laughter piercing the night like the peal of a bell.

Nights in occupied France were solemn, muted, for everyone. For us, they had to be totally silent. The silence was dark and heavy; it had heft, mass, the crushing weight of an elephant. When the sun went down, the silence lumbered in on great, padded feet. I dreaded night: Its arrival felt like a kind of death.

We became spare and deliberate in our movements. Words, when necessary, were whispered furtively. We tried to make the very blood in our veins slow down because it felt as if we could hear the sound of our hearts, their defiant pumping like a timpani in the tomb-like quiet. This was not living, it was surviving. Every noise was magnified after sundown. We could hear the scuttle of an insect across the floor, the burrowing sound of rats in the walls. The building itself made more noise than we did, sighing and settling around us. We tended to go to bed shortly after dusk to make the dawn come more quickly.

One night after dark, when I was already wedged between my brothers on our mattress and waiting for the sun to rise, we heard the sound of footsteps coming up the stairs. One pair of feet, climbing steadily. My parents sprung up from their mattress, and my brothers and I sat up too. The footsteps stopped on our landing and the doorknob rattled. Someone was fiddling with our locked door, trying to open it! I locked eyes on my father, half-lit by the moon, to see how he would respond. Who could that possibly be? No one should be coming into the warehouse. We were frozen, statues pointed toward the door. The knob was spinning and rattling; surely in a matter of moments the lock would give way and we would be exposed. I willed myself to be invisible and braced myself for whatever came next. And then ...

AAACHOOO! The sneeze burst forth from my mother with physical force, exploding from her body. She gasped in surprise and her hand immediately flew to her mouth to cover her traitorous lips. She looked at us in wide-eyed horror. *Now what?*

My father's arms shot out, hands starfish-splayed, directing us to stay as we were. We remained completely still, like stone sculptures in a moonlit cemetery. Through the open window, a police siren wailed in the distance. After a few very long seconds, seconds when our hearts pounded in our ears, we heard the slow scrape of shoes sliding back from our door, then the rapid descent as a man fled down the stairs and into the courtyard, walking quickly away across the cobblestones, and then, finally, the cold click of the metal gate closing behind him.

As the sound of his footsteps faded, we exhaled. Blood pounding in our ears, we whispered. *Who was that Papa? Who would be coming to our door at night?*

"It's okay," he reassured us, his voice cool and quiet. "These are hard times for everyone, and some people are desperate enough to resort to looting. Maybe he was looking for something he could steal and sell, or maybe he was just looking for food. But," and there was steel in his voice despite the whisper, "he wasn't looking for us."

The relief rose in us like a helium balloon, a rush of giddiness and light. We were safe, at least for now. I felt the hot needles of adrenaline all over my body, slow to fade. My brothers and I lay back down on our shared mattress, my head snug between their feet. I heard the sound of my parents settling in as well, and then the silence pressed down on us again, heavy and insistent. I tried to fall asleep, but my mind wandered. Why did that man come to our door, of all places? Madame Raymond locked the gates at sunset, leaving anyone who wanted to enter in the unfortunate position of having to ring the concierge's apartment, reaching someone likely to be grumpy at being summoned. Did the man sneak in before sunset and wait for his chance? Or was he someone who worked in the courtyard, who thought that he'd take advantage of the quiet to see what he could find? How did my father *know* that he was a looter? And, even if he was a burglar, what was to stop him from telling the police – perhaps in the hope of a reward – that they might want to visit a particular unit on the fourth floor of Stairway 6 at rue de Charonne because it might not be empty after all?

17

FALL 1942 – A NAZI IN THE COURTYARD

The work of a refinisher is quiet, almost meditative. In many of the woodworking trades, destruction precedes creation: Timber must be broken down before it can be transformed. By contrast, as my father explained, "Wood finishing is done gently. It's the delicate process of revealing the essential nature of wood." There's no strike of the hammer, no roar of the saw. At work, my father, a true master, looked like he was dancing with the wood. As he labored, there was the soft scritch, scritch, scritch, the faintest sound of sand meeting wood, like the rustle of a mouse. Most days, he worked from dawn to dusk. There was little else to do, and the work was keeping us alive – and probably keeping him sane.

Occasionally, we heard the muted sound of knuckles on the door behind the wardrobe, which meant Monsieur Thibou had furniture to deliver. We pushed the wardrobe away and his workers shouldered in the pieces in need of finishing, dropping them off and leaving without a word. Several items of furniture frequently were clustered together near the window of our already-crowded room.

One day, as I was peering out a window, standing on my tiptoes to try to get a better view, I felt my father's eyes on my back. The warehouse windows were smaller than our old apartment windows, which were floor-to-ceiling casements that, due to their ideal location, provided an almost complete view of the courtyard. These windows offered only a small glimpse of what was going on outside, and I had to wait for people to pass beneath them; it was like viewing the world from a spyhole. I'd just turned nine, it was summer, and I would normally be outside with Titi and other kids from the neighborhood, playing hide-and-seek throughout the stairways or bouncing a ball in the courtyard. I watched to see if any of them flew by. Nothing. I hoped, of course, to catch a glimpse of Titi, but I never did. Eventually, a dog, mud-brown and street-wise, wandered into view, his nose to the ground, looking for scraps. Behind me, I heard the sulfurous flare of a match as my father lit a cigarette.

"Goldener Kop, would you like me to teach you how to finish furniture?"

I turned to look at him. "Yes, Tatush!"

"Okay. The first step is to prepare the wood. Grab a scrap. Look for one that's flat, as smooth as possible." He nodded at our wood pile. "And I will show you how it's done." I picked up a small square block and my mother, who was darning our socks, smiled at me as I passed by her. "First, you must make a varnishing pad." He stubbed his cigarette out in the ashtray and rubbed his hands together. Also known as the tampon, the pad is the wood refinisher's most important tool. My father took a piece of cotton wool, folding it into a pyramid with one prominent point. It looked like a little woolen mouse. Then he took a piece of linen, the color of weak tea, and wrapped it around the wool, twisting the edges of the linen together into a pouch. With his other hand, using the meaty bit of his palm, he thumped firmly on the bottom of the linen pouch, flattening it.

"The bottom must be smooth or it will leave marks on the furniture. This tip," he said pointing to the face of the mouse, "is what we use to get into the smaller pieces. But this," – he turned up the flat, smooth bottom – "is what we use for the larger surfaces. Now let's make you one."

We took a smaller chunk of cotton wool, a smaller piece of linen cloth, to make it. Then he showed me how to wrap it, his hands so much more competent than mine, moving swiftly where mine stumbled. There were now two woolen mice: one large, one small. A sheriff and his deputy.

"In order to prepare the wood for the stain, you must first close the pores," he said. This is done with a solution that is a mixture of alcohol and pumice powder – the light gray volcanic rock turned to dust – that is poured directly onto the wood, like salt, "but just enough to make it damp, never wet." There was a gentle grinding sound as my father rubbed the solution into the top of a dresser, like the swish of a broom across the floor.

"How can you tell when it's ready?" I asked.

"By touch, by the way it feels when I touch it." Papa wiped his hands, little beads of sweat on his forehead. "It will take several days to dry, so we need to wait." Waiting was something I was getting a lot of practice at these days.

While we were waiting, the French Resistance was mobilizing. The previous fall, while Papa was imprisoned in Drancy, a civil servant named

Jean Moulin met with de Gaulle in London. In his first BBC address in June 1940, de Gaulle called for the French to keep fighting. His call had been answered. Throughout France, there were many different Resistance cells, all working independently with the same goal: to fight against the collaborationist Vichy régime and the Nazi occupation of France. To succeed, they needed to work together. De Gaulle was impressed with Moulin and subsequently charged him with the task of mobilizing the disparate Resistance *maquis* into a coherent Resistance organization, a daunting and dangerous task. Moulin, with his strong brow, large eyes, and a mouth that always hinted at a smile, fit the part of a dashing operative perfectly. On January 1, 1942, operating under the code name Max, Moulin parachuted into the craggy Alpilles mountains of Provence and set to work.

Weeks passed, and I continued to learn French polishing, taking countless irregular blocks from the scrap pile, carving a capital B into each one with my pocket knife. B for Bernard. B for Binem. When I worked next to my father, it was easy to forget about the world outside that I was missing: my friends, marbles, playing ball. Whatever my Papa did, I copied, inexpertly, on my own small block of wood. While one piece of furniture cured, my father moved to another. "This is the second stage," he said. "We are going to apply the polish."

I held up the jar of polish, swirling around the amber liquid, looking at the way the light played in it. The polish was the color of strong tea but smelled nothing like tea at all. It was sharp in my nose and burned my eyes when I sniffed it.

My father moved a polish-imbued pad on the wood, leaving a trail like a shooting star. "That's how you know it's working," he explained, pointing to the trail. "You never start or stop in the middle of the wood surface, as that will leave burn marks. Instead you go edge to edge. And if you press too hard, or if you go too fast, you will also burn the wood and spoil it. You have to be very gentle." After the first couple of coats, he added a few drops of linseed oil to the wood – the oil was the color of liquid sun – to alleviate the tackiness that started to appear on its surface. "Just a few drops," he cautioned, as he watched me do the same on my block of wood.

When the pad started to dry out, my father added a bit more of the shellac solution. It stained his hands as he worked: It was this mixture that, when I was younger, I used to peel off his hand at the end of each workday. Now my own hands were covered in taffy-like layers of shellac. After several coats, the furniture needed to rest overnight. My father put the pad in a jar and poured some alcohol over it so that it would remain damp. "We'll need to repeat this process three, maybe four times, until we build up the layers," he said. That was fine with me; there was nothing else to do.

An SS officer was in our courtyard. The Nazi stood quietly next to his car, an oil-black Mercedes that shone with a beautiful menace. His eyes scanned the area, taking in the people around him, the ateliers that surrounded the courtyard. He was alone, silent. Standing there in his impossibly crisp uniform, the officer seemed to be waiting for something. Or someone. While I was unaware of his presence, my father had registered it and was monitoring him closely.

It was mid-afternoon and I was lost in my woodwork, delicately tapping decorative detail into my latest woodblock. It was one of those days when the air hung heavy, teasing but not delivering the relief of rain. The two south-facing windows exposed our warehouse to a lot of sun but offered no cross-ventilation to bring relief. On cooler days, when there was a strong wind, sometimes air would push its way in anyway, but on days like today, the room was a fug of sweat and varnish.

I knelt on the floor, the backs of my knees slippery with sweat, completely oblivious that only a few feet away from me, my father had started tracking the SS officer. As I continued tap, tap, tapping away, Father was looking out the window almost obsessively, his head pivoting as if his eyes were tugged by invisible strings between the cabinet he was refinishing and the view out of the window.

Like me, my mother and Henri continued with their projects, also unaware of the officer in the courtyard. Papa didn't say a word, but eventually, pursing his lips and frowning, he set down his tools and gave up all pretense of work.

Why, my father silently wondered, was the Nazi officer there? He was out of place, but he did not seem lost. What was he waiting for? The SS officer was all starched clothes and shiny boots, and everything about his pristine appearance was out of place in our working-class courtyard, the buildings blotchy with flaking plaster and rain runoff, the workers rough-shaven and soiled by sweat. The effect was jarring, dissonant, like someone playing the wrong note in a familiar song. Tradesmen glanced at him as they passed, raised an eyebrow, exchanged meaningful looks with each other, and then went about their day. But their familiar movements had the heightened air of performance, the stilted manner of those who are aware they are being watched. Minutes passed. The clip-clop of hooves announced the arrival of a horse-drawn wagon with new wood for Monsieur Herbin. Someone dumped out a bucket of dirty water, the brown water running in rivers between the cobblestones.

I remained unaware of the rising tension, which was affecting not just my father but everyone around the courtyard who saw the officer. Careful not to let us know what was going on in his mind, my father was frantically trying to work out an escape plan. *Was it safer to wait, or should we flee now? Could he get us up the stairs and into the attic, where we could make our way to another stairway and possibly a different exit? Even if we could, where would we hide next? What would we take? When should he say something to my mother, to us?* With his heart banging against the cage of his chest, he somehow managed to maintain an impassive, neutral expression. He did not want us to panic. My father watched as the soldier paced in the courtyard. *Ten minutes.* The officer squinted up at the sun. He took his cap off, smoothed his hair. He tapped the cap against his leg, as if to the beat of a song in his head. *Fifteen minutes.* My father stared. The Nazi circled his car, eyed a pigeon that was strutting about nearby. Kicking at the air, he sent the bird bobbing away indignantly. *Twenty minutes.*

Though everyone was moving stiffly, most had no cause to be afraid. But we did, so my father continued watching, still as a statue. The afternoon sun hit our windows, and he hoped that the reflection was enough to transform the glass into mirrors, making it impossible for the Nazi to see inside. Then again, maybe the officer didn't need to see inside. Maybe he already knew we were there. Maybe we'd been discovered. Or betrayed.

Finally, after about 30 minutes, the Nazi officer was greeted by the courtyard mechanic, a jowled bulldog of a man who ran a shop on the ground floor of Stairway 8. The two spoke briefly, then the hood of the sedan went up, and the mechanic's top half disappeared behind it. *Ah, the officer is having car problems.* When the mechanic emerged, he pulled a rag from the pocket of his grease-stained coveralls and wiped his hands, pointing to something in the engine while the SS officer nodded. Soon the problem was fixed and the Mercedes drove away, with the officer behind the wheel. We were safe, for now.

Papa turned back from the window to face us, bringing an unlit Gauloise to his lips. If I'd looked closely at his hands, I'm sure I would have seen a slight tremor, the telltale signal of his rare quivering nerves. He cleared his throat loudly. "I thought we were about to be arrested," he said to the room, his manner as matter-of-fact as if he was making an observation about the weather. He told us about the German officer while we stared, taken aback, having had no idea of what unfolded outside our window. When the cigarette had burned down to a stub, he twisted it in the ashtray and rubbed his hands together, signifying that he was ready to move on.

"Binem," he said, holding up a new tampon, "we are ready for the last step. Come watch." The third and final step is where you remove the extra oils from the wood. For this last step, the tampon has only alcohol. "This is the most crucial step, because if you do it wrong, all of the work you've done to lead up to this is wasted. If you get sloppy at the end, everything is ruined." If there's one thing my father wasn't, it was sloppy. Not in his work and not in the way – always thinking ahead – he strove to keep us safe.

Though he'd told us about the officer, my father did not reveal how much the event had unnerved him. He hid his fears to not frighten any of us; he tucked his worries into the folds of his jacket and stuffed his darkest apprehensions into the pockets of his worn-out trousers. He was not a naturally self-contained man, and the continued stress of worrying about us was wearing on him. Unbeknownst to us, invisible cracks were forming, and, eventually, in the middle of the night, when we were most vulnerable, he would shatter.

18

WINTER 1942 – A NIGHT AT THE MOVIES

"Ah, you would not believe the lines in the Métro today," said Monsieur Roger. "It was so crowded that I had to let two trains pass before I could board. The first two were packed full of Boche soldiers, like sardines in a can." He pulled his arms in tight against his narrow body and sucked in his cheeks, apparently his version of a sardine, and then handed my father the newspaper and shrugged out of his coat.

Monsieur Roger was our window to the outside world. A slender, rough-shaven man about my father's age, he was a furniture maker who worked for one of Papa's clients. Like my father, he was strong, with lean, ropy limbs from days spent performing physical labor. He lived in the neighborhood with his wife, and he stopped to visit us almost every afternoon on his way home from work. We heard his special knock – a strange scraping sound he made with two knuckles – and he then entered with a newspaper tucked under his arm. All papers were under German influence and could not be trusted, but even tainted news was better than none.

Monsieur Roger picked up one of my wooden blocks and played with it absently while my mother poured him a glass of wine. "Ah, Henri," he looked up at my brother. "I am still searching for an earphone for you. I didn't think anything would be harder than the tin foil, but ..." he shrugged, trailing off.

Henri had the idea to make a crystal radio, also known as a *radio à galèn* or foxhole radio. The simple radio, which gets its name from the lead sulfide galena crystal, does not require electricity; instead, it gets its power from the radio waves themselves picked up via a long antenna. Monsieur Roger had told us about de Gaulle's BBC broadcasts, and Henri wanted to see if we could listen to the radio from the warehouse. Monsieur Roger was helping to find the materials for him, but the search was proving harder than anticipated.

"That's all right, Monsieur Roger," Henri joked. "It's not like we're going anywhere."

Monsieur Roger chuckled in acknowledgment and pivoted to my father. "Monsieur Parkiet," he said, "take a look at the article about the Germans moving south into the so-called unoccupied zone." He accepted the wine from my mother and passed her his coat; she lay it across our mattress and pulled out a chair – our only chair – so he could sit. Lowering himself with a groan, he continued, "If you believe the paper, it's because France and Germany are great friends, best friends even." He rolled his eyes. "*Bêtise* [Nonsense]!"

The Germans moved into southern France in November 1942, assuming control of Vichy France in response to the Allied invasion of northern Africa where the Vichy government had been overseeing the French colonies. In occupying southern France, Germany also hoped to gain control of the demobilized French naval fleet, docked in Toulon. However, the French naval commanders scuttled the entire fleet, preferring to have the battleships and submarines sink into the turquoise waters of the Mediterranean. While Hitler was disappointed to lose the ships, he was pleased at least that de Gaulle would not get his hands on them, either.

Most days, Monsieur Roger stayed only a few minutes, just long enough to drink his wine and share the news with us before heading home to his wife. To my knowledge, neither of my parents drank alcohol – and they certainly never drank wine, which was a staple of the French diet. Even so, we always had wine in the apartment; my father must have sensed it was a nice social gesture, and even now, while in hiding, I was regularly sent across the street to the *marchand de vin* [wine merchant] with a deerskin carafe slung over my shoulder, handing over black-market ration tickets, to maintain the tradition of hospitality. Occasionally, Monsieur Roger would stay longer and have a second glass. On those days, his cheeks bloomed with warmth and he told us stories – or rather, the same story – about his capture and torture by the Germans. He was never clear on the reason for his detention, but he was always sure to stress the details of his heroism.

"You know, boys, I am a communist," he would begin, leaning forward in his chair. "A communist believes everyone is equal, and what is wrong with that?" He looked us each in the eye, daring us to argue.

"Hitler doesn't believe everyone is equal, though," he said, taking a sip of wine. "No, he doesn't." He paused, looking out the window with a distant, dreamy cast in his eyes. "Yes, communists believe that people like us – like your father and myself, men who work hard for a living – should have more of a say in how the world is run.

"I'm no friend of the Nazis. And that's why they tortured me, that's why they tried to get me to share everything I know with them. But did I say anything? Did I break? No, I did not!"

We had heard this story many times. After all, we were literally a captive audience.

"And why not?! Because I am a man!" *Je suis un homme!* He pounded his chest with each word.

Satisfied he had made his point, he pulled out a tin of tobacco. I loved to watch him roll cigarettes. He was missing the last two fingers from his right hand: An accident with a saw had left him with a hand like a lobster claw. But he rolled cigarettes with admirable dexterity, using just the two fingers and thumb to twirl the tobacco back and forth in its paper canoe rapidly until it was ready. He then licked the paper, moistening the glue, closed it with his tongue, and placed the cigarette between his thin lips.

He smoked while enjoying the last of his wine and then passed the empty glass to my mother as he stood to leave. "Thank you for the wine, Madame and Monsieur Parkiet," Monsieur Roger said. "I'll see you tomorrow."

Monsieur Roger didn't know Yiddish, so he spoke to my parents in a sort of pidgin French that they could understand. To my brothers and me, he spoke a common French, as you would to a native, and my parents could not always follow the conversation. But there was no mistaking him when he loudly proclaimed, "Je suis un homme!" Even my mother understood him quite clearly and, behind his back, she gently rolled her eyes. Sometimes we pretended to be Monsieur Roger after he'd gone; Mama was often the most enthusiastic, making her voice low and thumping her own chest for emphasis as she strode around our small space.

We laughed a bit at Monsieur Roger's expense, but we were immensely grateful for his visits and company. He took a significant risk because those who aided Jews, even if they were simply aware of their existence and failed to turn them in, became, in the eyes of the Germans, no better than Jews themselves. Had he been caught, Monsieur Roger would almost have certainly ended up in Drancy and perhaps Auschwitz. So there is no question that Monsieur Roger was doing us a great service by visiting each day. He came to see us because he cared about us and hated the Germans. But he also came for the wine.

Monsieur Roger was our most frequent guest but not the only one. When the cured ham was whittled down to the white of the bone, a young man in suspenders arrived from the country to replace it. On rare occasions, he brought eggs. When our hair grew so long that it fell into our eyes, the small, serious barber from down the street appeared at the warehouse with his little black barber bag and gave us a trim, my mother sweeping up the hair as it drifted to the ground. Monsieur Malé and his son Guy, residents of the top floor of Stairway 8 and the nearest permanent inhabitants, were occasional visitors, too. Monsieur Malé was a government employee and Guy, a teenager, was attending lycée [high school]. One day, Guy appeared at the warehouse with a stack of books and a pencil tucked behind his ear. He offered to tutor me so I didn't fall behind. We sat on the floor with our legs crossed, reviewing the rules of French grammar and solving math problems together.

As the months went by, Guy's visits became less and less frequent until eventually, he stopped coming altogether. The pull of his own life was probably too strong, and while I can't imagine he forgot we were there, I suspect it was hard to keep us in his thoughts, hidden away as we were, ossifying in our warehouse hideaway. No doubt Guy and his father must have wondered if things would ever be different. The Germans governed Paris, and they showed no sign of changing their antisemitic policies. We couldn't hide forever. We were waiting, but for what? For France to come to its senses? For someone to rescue us? But what if no one did? Then we were as good as dead – dusty relics of a time gone by, perhaps never to be brought back to life.

It was New Year's Eve and Monsieur Roger asked my parents if they would allow me to join him and his wife at the nearby movie theater. "Everyone will be celebrating," he tipped back an invisible drink with a wink, "and no one will be in the mood to arrest anyone. We'd bring our own child if we had one but," he paused to smile down at me, giving me an affectionate squeeze, "he could easily be our boy. It will be safe."

My parents were unsure at first since gendarmes and German soldiers regularly stopped civilians to check identification papers and would certainly probe if anything seemed off. However, New Year's Eve was a night that even the SS would celebrate, so the risk was deemed an acceptable one.

As we walked out the door, I looked back and waved at my family. My father stood next to my mother, his hand on her shoulder. I was excited to go out, but it also felt odd leaving the warehouse, particularly to see a movie without my father. Seeing movies together was something he and I shared, just the two of us, and my heart felt a tug as I left him behind.

We exited 5 rue de Charonne and turned right onto the much busier rue du Faubourg Saint-Antoine. Already this was farther than I'd been in months, and we were just steps from our courtyard. I walked between Monsieur and Madame Roger as we made our way down the street, weaving in and out of the other celebrants. It was a cold night and I wore one of Henri's old coats, the sleeves rolled up because it was too big. Music poured out of cafés and bistros, and inside, people laughed and danced the *bal-musette* [French accordion music], couples pressed together and swaying in tight circles. The world was alive out here. All of Paris seemed drunk on revelry, yet I was acutely aware that back in the warehouse, my family was sitting in the cold, silent dark.

At Place de la Bastille we made another right turn and passed a group of Wehrmacht with their dates, waving champagne bottles and singing as they walked. We were taking a route that I'd walked dozens of times before with my father, holding his stump of a finger. The glowing orbs of the streetlights brightened the dark street and reminded me how long it had been since I'd been outside at night. Madame Roger took my hand as we walked past the soldiers; her leather glove was cold and I could smell her sandalwood perfume.

We turned right onto Boulevard Richard-Lenoir and were at the Bastille-Palace theater. The movie was the *La Fille du Piaster* [The Well-Digger's Daughter], a romantic comedy melodrama set in the early days of World War II. Patricia, the daughter of the well-digger, is a beautiful and naive girl who is seduced by a rakish pilot, a wealthy and handsome fellow accustomed to breaking hearts. He is unexpectedly called to service, leaving so suddenly that he fails to appear for their next rendezvous. However, she is left with something of his: an unborn child. Disgraced and cast out by her father, she is resigned to raising her child on her own, all while the military reports that the pilot is missing, presumed dead. Amid this tragedy are long moments of comic relief, provided by the great comic actor Fernandel, with his expressive features and large, horse-like teeth. Fernandel plays Felipe, another well-digger who, at one point, gets riotously drunk and acts the fool, much to the delight of a crowd of watching villagers. In the dark of the theater, we laughed at Felipe's buffoonery and were delighted when, in the end, the pilot reappears – alive after all! – and he and Patricia marry. For those two hours, I was transported to another place and, though I missed my father sitting next to me – the scent of his Gauloises, the sound of his low chuckles in the dark – I was immensely happy to be in a movie theater again.

When I got back home, I acted out bits of the movie for my father, my breath making clouds in the unheated warehouse. Feeling protected by the rowdy celebration that raged on outside the courtyard, we risked making noise, me staggering around, my father laughing as I pretended to be the drunken clown. It was a particularly cold night, with ice crystals on the windows, and as we got ready for bed, we put on all available clothing, emptying the armoire of each garment until, layer after layer, our limbs were stuffed like sausages into our clothes. Barely able to move, we put our coats on last and got under our blankets. While the rest of Paris celebrated until the wee hours, we huddled together like rabbits in an underground warren.

19

SPRING 1943 – MILICIEN

Time continued to move on without us. In January 1943, President Roosevelt and Prime Minister Churchill met on the outskirts of Casablanca, Morocco. Inside the Anfa Hotel, an art deco property that looked like a massive cruise ship, the leaders discussed military strategy and developed plans to invade Italy. De Gaulle and Henri Giraud were also in attendance, both quietly vying to be recognized by the Allies as the legitimate leader of France in exile. FDR held a particular antipathy toward de Gaulle, preferring Giraud, and by this time even Churchill had wearied of his French guest and outsized ego. Yet de Gaulle, who had the firm support of the French Resistance, was considered essential to the cause.

In Paris, the city's population took another dip. Not only were Jews and foreigners still being deported, but new regulations required young Frenchmen to enlist in the *Service du travail obligatoire* [Compulsory Work Service] and travel to Germany as forced labor. With Nazi Germany having sent its young men to the Eastern Front, hundreds of thousands of Frenchmen provided much-needed manpower, living in work camps and toiling away in German factories.

I missed my friends. I missed being outside. With few options available for entertainment, I did the same things over and over. I continued to refinish wood blocks, tapping a decorative B into each one using a pin and hammer. I whittled wood scraps, the paper-thin shavings flitting to the ground like the wings of dead insects. My mother taught me to knit French style and I made a cord from the small length of yarn she could spare. The cord dangled from the end of the wooden spool like a hangman's noose;

once I reached the end of the yarn, I unwound the cord and began again. Like Penelope weaving and unweaving the burial shroud for Odysseus, I worked and then erased my work, my fingers becoming as calloused and pinpricked as those of an expert tailor.

Mostly I continued to stare out the window and dream of freedom. In one recurring daydream, I am riding out of the courtyard on the bare back of a donkey with Titi behind me, her arms wrapped around my waist, our bare legs swinging slowly with each step. Her brown curls glimmer like topaz in the sun. We wave as we pass the admiring courtyard workers, neighbors, and friends and head through the courtyard entrance and into the wider world beyond.

One spring evening, after the day workers had left, we heard a noise through the wall we shared with Monsieur Thibou's shop. A loud crash, the reverberations of which echoed in the courtyard. The sound of two men shouting, and another loud crash. We were eating dinner, sitting cross-legged on the floor around our short makeshift table, quietly slurping soup. We paused at the sound of fighting. Noise like this would bring unwanted attention. What should we do? Should we wait and hope for the best? The shouting continued, getting louder. Should we go downstairs and then up Stairway 5 to knock on Monsieur Thibou's door? It was too risky. We might be seen coming out of Stairway 6.

As the yelling intensified, Papa waved Severin over and the two of them pushed the armoire away from the connecting door. Then, straining further, Papa edged the bookcase forward that blocked the entrance from the other side. Light flooded in from the shop and we saw Monsieur Thibou and Monsieur Grósz arguing furiously. The two men stood just inches apart, shouting at each other, spittle flying between them. Monsieur Thibou towered over the stocky, bull-necked Monsieur Grósz, but it was Grósz who appeared to be the aggressor, leaning forward, his index finger jabbing into Thibou's chest, mouth curled into a snarl over his toothbrush mustache. The men glanced at us briefly. Monsieur Thibou's eyes seemed to hold a glint of apology, but otherwise, neither man paid attention to us. Were they arguing about us? About the danger that came with harboring us? Maybe. I can't actually remember what they were arguing about; I don't think I even understood it in the moment. All I could focus on, all I felt, was the sharp fear that had me frozen in place.

Swiftly, my mother slipped into the shop and inserted herself between Monsieur Thibou and his partner. If they were going to get at each other, they would have to go through her, a tiny woman in a faded black dress with big, solemn eyes. Her concern that our family would be exposed overrode her typical sense of restraint and propriety. Mama took Monsieur Thibou's hand in hers, patting it softly.

"*S'il vous plaît,*" she entreated. "Please. Please. Please." It was a plea, a prayer. "You will bring the police. Please calm down." She whispered it as if by being quiet she could make them quiet, too. She pivoted to Monsieur Grósz now and took his hand, repeating the same plea while my father stood back with us, watching. "S'il vous plaît. S'il vous plaît."

Gradually, it worked. The men, perhaps ashamed that they were shouting before an entire panicked family and being confronted and implored by this small, shy woman, quieted down. Monsieur Thibou apologized, and Monsieur Grósz, still red-faced and angry, slammed the door as he departed in a huff. We retreated to the warehouse and Monsieur Thibou pushed the bookshelf back in front of the shop door, while on our side, Papa and Severin quietly nudged the armoire into its proper place. Once again, we were in a dark silence, sealed off from the shop, and from the world.

Days passed, and it seemed clear that no one had heard the argument, or at least that it had not brought the attention we feared. Monsieur Thibou came through the interior doorway to apologize once again and reassure us that he didn't think anyone had made note of anything unusual. Of course, there were other ways that we could be discovered and arrested. Just as I could feel the taut vibrations in the air start to settle, just as I could sense my parents starting to relax, Madame Raymond arrived at the warehouse with bad news. It was well known that opportunistic individuals could make money by turning in Jews to the authorities, and it turns out there was such an individual working in our courtyard. He was a carpenter who joined the *Milice française,* or French militia, for extra money. We didn't know him personally, but he knew about us, and he had a plan.

I emerged from the tunnel at the entrance into our long courtyard and moved purposefully, just as my father had instructed. Several wrapped brown paper packages from our neighbors' shops were under my left arm, pressed against my body. In my right hand, I carried our blue-and-white speckled pitcher, now filled with frothy milk. On a typical day I would spin the pitcher around while I sauntered, trying to delay, only for a moment or two, my return to the warehouse. But today my father had put me on high alert, so I was eager to return to safety.

"Look for someone younger than me. A bit taller," he had warned me as he held his hand several inches above his head. "Short brown hair. Clean-shaven. Someone you don't know, exactly, but who may seem familiar."

"That describes almost all of the people down there," Henri said, looking out the window to the men working below.

I registered the flicker of frustration on my father's face. Or maybe it was fear and concern. He sighed. "Binem, it's most important to be aware if someone is watching you closely. If they seem to be watching where you are going."

"Ok, Papa," I said with all the confidence I could muster, but Henri was right. All the tradesmen dressed similarly, in loose, practical pants and worn buttoned shirts, and they rotated through the courtyard frequently. We could identify only a fraction of the men who worked here, although many more were regulars we had never gotten to know.

Now I stopped briefly in the mouth of the courtyard and I looked around, scanning the scene before me to see if anyone looked like they might be watching me. It was busy, as usual. Someone was talking to Monsieur Herbin in front of Stairway 2 while he stood, his typical frown on his face, hands on his hips. Across from him and to my left, near Stairway 12, was a man stacking unfinished walnut planks. A cap hung low over his head, blocking his eyes. Was he watching me? I glanced to my right, toward Stairway 1. No one I knew was outside, and I felt a pang of longing, a powerful urge to enter and go up to my old apartment. Home. Except it wasn't our home anymore.

I looked back at the man in the cap. He had finished stacking and was turned away, getting his cart ready to leave. *Okay, he doesn't seem dangerous.* Near him another tradesman knelt, tying his bootlaces. He wiped his nose with his sleeve, then looked up and stared straight into my eyes. I flushed, startled. It seemed as if his eyes narrowed and locked in on me as if to say, *There you are. I've been looking for you.* My heart plummeted into my stomach.

I pivoted quickly to my right and walked directly into Stairway 2, scrambling up two flights of stairs, the milk splashing in the pitcher. Pausing on the second-floor landing, I peered down the center of the spiral staircase. *Is he following me?* I couldn't tell. My heart was pounding as I went up a few more steps, stopping in front of an unmarked door: the communal toilet. I looked up through the stairway. At the very top floor landing a wooden ladder ascended into the attic. *Should I keep going, into the attic?* I glanced at the pitcher – it would be difficult to climb the ladder with it, and I imagined the milk sloshing over the sides of the pitcher, splattering on the floor. A mess. Wasted food. Most importantly, evidence of where I'd gone.

Should I go back down to the basement? The dank of the cellar, the darkness that brought its own sort of terror? No. It didn't seem wise, I'd risk being seen. *Wait. Footsteps!* Someone was coming up the stairs! I ducked into the toilet and latched the lock.

The darkness was broken by daylight that framed the door. A rectangular ventilation grate in the door served as a kind of peephole, letting in additional light. I straddled the pit toilet and tried to ignore the sharp smell of urine while I took rapid, shallow breaths. Flies buzzed around me, excited by the scent of the food I was carrying. I strained, listening for the sound of further footsteps, but all I could hear was my own thumping heart and, in the distance, the sound of tradesmen shouting orders to each other in the courtyard. Sweat ran down in little rivulets from my forehead, stinging my eyes. A fly landed on my nose and I blew air upward, trying to dislodge it.

I pictured my parents back in the warehouse, starting to worry. My mother looking out the window, rocking back and forth with her arms wrapped, cradling her body. My father standing next to her, his fingers tapping the windowsill with nervous energy as he tried to reassure her. *I'm sure he's simply being careful like I told him to be. Probably taking one of his longer routes home.* My father would sound calm – he was implacable in the face of someone else's fear and good at not showing his own fear – but I knew he would be worried, too.

Still straddling the toilet, I continued to wait and listen. *Just pretend you're playing hide-and-seek*, I told myself. *Like you used to all the time.* How I wished I was simply playing a game of hide-and-seek now. That it was Titi who might find me and not a *milicen*.

I used to play hide-and-seek (*cache-cache*) almost every day after school. Kids came from all over the neighborhood to play in our courtyard. With its long, open interior and set of 13 interconnected stairways, it was one of the best places in the entire 11th arrondissement to play. The seeker would stand in the center of the yard, eyes covered, counting slowly to 100 while everyone else – the hiders – sprinted away to find suitable places to hole up.

I knew the labyrinthian corridors of 5 rue de Charonne better than just about anyone, making me excellent at cache-cache. I knew which stairs squeaked, which doors – the wood swollen due to improper curing – would stick; which neighbors were quick to be annoyed by the tumbling of kids, and which ones found it charming and might help you hide.

The basement was a good hiding place, though I didn't like being there alone. Sometimes Titi and I took a candle and explored the interconnected cellars, navigating them as though they were catacombs, the underground quarries that thread below Paris. With each step, we both hoped and feared that the candle might go out and we'd have to fumble in the darkness to light it. Occasionally we'd blow it out intentionally, a test of bravery, the fear more endurable because we were together, arms interlocked.

My favorite place to hide was the attic because it was the easiest way to get to any other area in the building, into any of the stairways you wanted, and I knew my way around there better than anyone else. The attic held a sense of mystery, its stale air smelling of forgotten furniture and once-prized knickknacks in rodent-chewed boxes. Up there I could hear the voices of people in the ateliers below, the conversations fading in and out on a ghostly tide. The scent of cigarettes, wood, and varnish drifted up through the rafters. I'm sure those on the fifth floor could hear me too, as I clambered along on my hands and knees above them.

Now I was hiding again. Alone. This time, hide-and-seek had much bigger consequences.

I heard muffled footsteps coming up the stairs. *Is he looking for me?* Blood pounded in my ears. A pair of boots climbed the staircase methodically, growing closer. The buzzing of the flies was so loud that it seemed like it would give me away, that they were shouting out my location. But the boots kept going, past me and up the stairs. I heard a door open one floor up, the murmur of a greeting. The door closed. Still, I stayed in the toilet, straddling the drain and trying to breathe quietly. I started to count in my head. *One. Two. Three.* I counted until I reached 100, as if I were the seeker, not the hider. The stairway was still silent and my heart started to slow; even the flies settled, bored of their game. *Ok, I think it's time to leave.* I opened the door cautiously and peeked out, still half expecting someone to be waiting for me, but the staircase was empty. At the entrance to the courtyard I paused, surveying the yard. The man I'd seen was gone. Everyone was busy, and no one was paying any attention to me. Before I could be noticed, I bolted to Stairway 6, to the warehouse.

Once inside I was encircled by my parents, with my brothers right behind them. They'd all been as terrified as I was. "I thought I saw the milicien, Papa." Now that I was safe, I felt my lips quiver, near tears. "I thought he was following me." My bravery dissolved and I melted into my mother's arms. I was home, or what passed for it these days.

My mother patted me all over as if looking for blood or bruising. "What happened? Are you okay?"

I explained what I'd seen, that I didn't know if it had been the milicien, but I'd been afraid. My father nodded and said, "Good job, Goldener Kop, you did the right thing."

Several days later, Monsieur Thibou stopped by. He stood with my father near the door, his lefthand jingling coins in his pants pocket, the tink, tink, tink of them louder than his whispered words so I couldn't hear what he was saying. More adults whispering in corners. I watched their expressions and tried to figure out what was going on. My father raised his eyebrows and held up his right palm, seemingly surprised by what Monsieur Thibou was telling him. Thibou's hands pressed together in front of his mouth as if in prayer, index fingers tapping together while he nodded. A frown from my father, then a small smile. More whispering. Thibou nodded again. My father smiled wider and, finally, shook Monsieur Thibou's hand.

Papa turned to us after Monsieur Thibou left. "We don't need to worry about the milicien any longer," Papa said. "It's been taken care of." He said it with a look of finality: We weren't to discuss this anymore. There would be no further details. But I had questions – questions I knew not to ask. Taken care of? What did that mean? Had someone left a stack of francs in an envelope, promising more if he stayed silent? Pulled him aside, yanked him up by his collar, and threatened him? Had one of our friends, some of whom were connected to the growing Resistance, held a knife to his throat, the cold metal against the hot pulse of his neck? Spilled his blood and left his body floating in the Seine? To this day, I don't know.

20

SUMMER 1943 – A DAY IN THE SUN

On a hot afternoon in July, Monsieur Weber, who was a family acquaintance, visited the warehouse. Monsieur Weber was a Hungarian Jew, but he was not hiding from the Germans – he didn't have to. In the beginning, not all Jews in France had to hide. Germany and Hungary were allies in World War II, which meant that Jews from Hungary were not immediate targets of the anti-Jewish policies enacted by the Nazis in France; they were protected by the Axis alliance. Hungarian Jews were not arrested during the early roundups, although they had to comply with many of the antisemitic regulations, including the requirement to wear the yellow star. It's not that Hungary loved its Jewish citizens – antisemitism was rampant there – but the country, perhaps out of nationalistic pride, was nevertheless reluctant to deport them, despite continual pressure from Germany to do so. Because of this alliance, the Hungarian Jews in France were likewise safe. For a while.

Monsieur Weber offered Papa a cigarette and the two men spoke quietly. Then Monsieur Weber turned and smiled at me through a cloud of smoke. Would I like to have a picnic on the Marne River with him and Madame Weber? I looked eagerly at my father. Absolutely I would.

That Sunday I waited by the window, my legs bouncing in anticipation. Papa and Severin were sharing the most recent newspaper, with Severin sprawled out on our bed with his portion. Henri sat cross-legged on the floor in front of the low table, building his crystal radio. Monsieur Roger had finally succeeded in finding an earpiece, and now Henri was studiously coiling wire into a makeshift capacitor. I'd been sitting next to him, watching him work, but I was so excited, and a little bit nervous, that I kept fidgeting and bumping into the table.

"Bernard, stop it, you are making the table move!" Henri snapped. "This is hard enough without you knocking into it." So I went to the window and watched until I saw Monsieur Weber's fedora bobbing below. He took his hat off as he entered from the hallway; he greeted everyone warmly, nodding and smiling as if it were a normal social call and not a visit to a family in hiding. Severin put down his paper and Henri looked up from his radio. Did they wish they were joining me? It didn't occur to me then – I was self-absorbed in the way all children are – but I wonder now how much they must have longed to be outside in the sun. If they felt jealous, they never let me feel it.

"Are you ready Bernard?" Monsieur Weber looked down at me and smiled widely, his round cheeks even more pronounced than usual. "My wife is waiting across the street." He looked at my parents. My father stood with his arm around my mother. She was smiling, but her eyes looked worried. "She sends her regards to all of you. We wish you could join us. Hopefully this will not last much longer."

We took the Métro to the last stop on Line 8, Charenton-le-Pont station, and from there walked almost two kilometers, the picnic basket thumping awkwardly against Monsieur Weber's thigh with each step, to the L'ile de Charentonneau. At the riverbank, Madame Weber unfurled a faded woolen blanket with a gentle snap, and we spread the blanket in the sun. The wool tickled the back of my legs, but I didn't mind because the sun felt like the hug of a beloved, long-absent relative. I was pale and sun-starved and as I lay back on the blanket and closed my eyes, I could feel the sun's gaze, warming and breathing life into me.

It was a gorgeous, technicolor afternoon. A rowboat drifted by, its wake spreading like the train of a wedding gown. Next to us, a couple was laughing at a private joke, their bodies forming an A as they leaned into each other. My nostrils were filled with the herbaceous scent of grass, as rich and tantalizing as food. Nearby a toddler, not yet master of his own legs, staggered down the sloped bank until his mother caught his hand and walked him back up the hill. At the top of the grassy mound they posed for a photo, the boy's father kneeling while his mother attempted to coax the toddler into standing still. I was reminded of many Sundays at the park with my father, posing for similar photos.

My father had purchased a camera at a time when owning one was still a rarity, particularly among working-class families like ours. He beamed with excitement when he brought it home, lifting the new Kodak out of the cardboard box gingerly, cradling it like a newborn. Papa studied the simple box camera, which was made of bakelite and smelled of formaldehyde, while Henri and Severin watched closely over his shoulder. My father was for the most part a frugal, practical man and at the time this must have seemed an extravagant purchase.

On Sundays our family went for long walks in one of the city's many parks, grand verdant respites from the urban environment we lived in Monday through Saturday. The photos of my childhood are almost exclusively from these weekend adventures. Me bundled in a stroller in the Jardin du Luxembourg next to a cousin, both of us toddlers. Me wearing a crisp newsboy cap and a dark sweater, standing on a slatted folding chair so I am almost as tall as my mother, who stands next to me and squints into the camera. Me standing solemnly with my brothers, hands behind my back, in front of a statue in the Jardin des Plantes – the immense botanical garden founded in 1626 to grow medicinal herbs for Louis XIII. "Ah, I've got it now – boys, move closer to one another – Henek, don't pinch your brother! That's it, stand still. Good, good, just a moment more," Papa coaxed. Even now when I look at that photo I remember the restlessness my brothers and I felt at having to pose, trying to remain motionless, when all we wanted to do was run around and play. Pictures from these and other outings were among my family's most precious belongings; in July 1942, when we briefly stole back into our apartment to gather our mattresses and other essentials, my father made sure to grab the photo album.

At the edge of the Marne River, a boy about my age held a toy sailboat on the water, watching it bob up and down. I leaned back on my elbows, watching him a bit enviously and remembering all the Sundays I'd spent at Jardin du Luxembourg racing my own sailboat. It was a very French pastime, and even today, if you visit the park on any pleasant afternoon, you are sure to find many children there, sailing boats or throwing corn to the ducks that float by. I'd lean over the wide cement edge of the basin and push my sailboat away with a bamboo stick, watching as it left a trail of silken ripples. "Go, go, go!" I'd whisper words of encouragement, willing the boat to sail to the other side but worried that it would falter in the middle of the basin, become adrift, and be lost to me forever. When the sails caught wind and gathered speed, I'd dash around to the other side and catch it before it bumped into the concrete rim. I wondered where that boat was now, if it was still waiting for me in our old apartment, or if the gendarmes had taken it the day my father watched them carrying away all our belongings.

I thought of my mother back in our room, the dark half-moons under her eyes as she bent over her sewing. She spent her days rotating through the same set of chores: cooking, mending, and cleaning out the chamber pot, never leaving our hiding place. Before the war, my mother loved our family walks on Sundays and particularly loved looking at the flowers in the parks. Her favorite park was the Jardin des Plantes. As my parents strolled its wide *allées* [paths], shaded by the wall of plane trees, my brothers and I dashed among them, sun-dappled and laughing while Mama bent to inspect the meticulously tended roses, the delicate pink peonies, the orange tulips shaped like tea cups. So many colors!

It was so different from what she was used to growing up in Warsaw. It was as if when God made the world, He started in France when His palette was filled with every color in the rainbow. He painted each detail with intense precision, from the flame-kissed dahlias to the impossibly iridescent blue stripes on the wings of the Eurasian jays. But by the time He made His way east to Poland, the colors on His once crisp palette had run together into a pigment as gray and drab as porridge, and He covered Warsaw in wide, somber swaths of dullness, eager to be done with His task.

Mama taught me about the flowers; she told me that some opened up each morning to bathe in the sun and then closed down again at night, their petals curling in on themselves like a shield. She explained that the sun made them grow, giving life to everything green around me. Sitting by the riverbank, looking at the ruddy, happy faces of the people around me, I wondered, Did people need the sun in the same way that plants did? I thought of the pale faces of my family and how diminished we seemed by the past year. Were we wilting? Deprived of the sun's gaze, were we slowly dying in that small room?

Madame Weber unwrapped lunch, a wartime version of *túrós csusza*, a sweet Hungarian noodle dish traditionally made with cheese and jam. "It's not made as I would have liked – it's impossible to find ingredients these days – but it is still one of our favorites." At the first bite my mouth awoke, flooded with flavors. "Madame," I said, "I think this is the best thing I've ever tasted!" I meant it: After a year of salted ham, I'd forgotten what it was like to taste something sweet. I slurped up as much as I could while trying to remain reasonably polite. Madame Weber clucked in appreciation at my appetite and patted my leg. I lay back on the blanket again, my cheeks sticky and my belly full, and we watched the boats go by. I picked at the grass absently, rubbing the moist stems between my thumb and forefinger so that my fingers were stained green. It smelled so fresh that I wanted to take some of that freshness home. I put a handful of grass and a yellow wildflower into my pocket.

I squinted at Monsieur Weber. He had a round face and the nose of a pugilist, bent slightly off-center. I narrowed my eyes more and his features began to blur, as if viewed through a rain-covered window, and I could almost pretend he was my father. Looking at Madame Weber this same way,

I could pretend it was my mother's small hands patting my knee instead of Madame's meaty ones, that it was my mother sitting with her knees folded under her, wrapping up the remnants of our lunch. Monsieur and Madame Weber had no children of their own; despite their wishes, they had not been so fortunate. As I pretended that my parents were here with me, perhaps the Webers pretended they were with their own child. To the rest of the world, we were a Hungarian family out for a Sunday picnic. The thought made my throat constrict, a knot of sadness coming to rest under my jaw, hard and heavy like a marble, and I was overcome with longing for my family, with the wish they could leave the warehouse and be here with me.

The day began to cool. Madame Weber picked flecks of grass off the blanket and I helped her fold it. We walked back to the train station, part of a trail of people snaking their way back to the city, sluggish and drowsy from the sun. The picnic basket, now lighter, thumped quietly against Monsieur Weber's leg. Monsieur Weber escorted me into my courtyard and we climbed the stairs to my door together. After a quick hello to my parents, he left, and I chattered nonstop for the next hour or so about the day that had left my cheeks blooming from the sun.

As dusk turned into night, the buildings outside our window disappeared into the darkness. After eating our usual meager dinner, we extinguished the candle and settled into silence. I lay on the mattress, surrounded by the animal warmth of my brothers and the mushroomy scent of their feet. I tried to hold on to the fresh green scent of the Marne, but the musty smell of my mattress and the stuffiness of the small room made it seem like everything was decomposing around me.

I thought of that day for weeks, long after the grass in my pockets had faded into desiccated wisps and the yellow flower had shriveled into a tiny, dead sun. Having briefly tasted freedom, I felt more than ever like a prisoner within the pigeon-gray walls of our courtyard, and our dim, colorless room seemed even smaller than before. Hours stretched by. I carved my initials into wood. I varnished the blocks until they were as dark and shiny as a beetle. I knit coil after coil of yarn and I reread the two picture books that remained from my short-lived study sessions with Guy. I stared at the type on the page until the words were as meaningless to me as hieroglyphs, little black ants marching in a line. I flipped through the pictures, always coming to rest at my favorite.

In it, a car winds up a mountainside road, away from the viewer. A mountain wall rises sharply on the left side of the road; on the other side, the cliff drops off. There are craggy peaks in the distance and the car is about to drive around a curve and disappear from view. I traced the bend of the road with my finger, mapping out the ridged crests of those mountains with the focus of a topographer. Some days, I created stories about where the car was heading and who was in it. Mostly, I stared into the picture as if willing it to draw me into the car. In this way, the hours, days, and months crawled past.

I never saw Monsieur or Madame Weber again. After Germany terminated its alliance with Hungary in March 1944, they disappeared. Now their names are etched in stone on The Wall of Names at the Shoah Memorial.

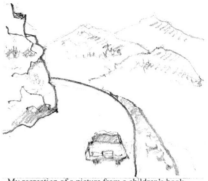

My recreation of a picture from a children's book
I read over and over while in hiding.

21

SPRING 1944 – NEW NEIGHBORS

The water started out warm, but by now it was cold and gray with dirt. I was standing in front of the potbelly stove, the front half of my body toasted by the fire and the back covered in goosebumps. I cleaned myself quickly with a cloth. "Why do I have to do this? We don't go anywhere. We don't see anyone. Who cares if we are dirty?" I said this with the half-hearted protest of someone who knows that complaint is futile.

"It's important to keep our bodies clean and healthy," my mother tutted in response as she set down a fresh bowl of water at my feet and dropped the washcloth into the bowl.

Before the war, my brothers would go to the *bains-douches municipaux* [public baths and showers] with Papa each Wednesday where, according to Henri, the water was always warm, hot if you wanted it to be. The bains-douches were a short stroll away on rue du Faubourg St. Antoine and I watched enviously when they left. I was too young to join them; instead, my weekly bath was a basin filled with water and, just like now, the water cooled far too quickly for my liking.

Back then I was young enough that my mother bathed me while I stood near our sink, frowning at my feet and the dirt stuck in the creases of my toes. Most days, I came home covered in sand because I spent my afternoons crawling in the sandboxes of the Place des Vosges. My toenails stared back at me like little blank faces while Mama lifted my arm and wiped sand crystals from the folds of my armpits. It always tickled and I scooted away. "I don't know how you manage to get sand in these places," my mother would say, shaking her head.

While I played under the shade of the elm trees, my mother watched from a nearby bench, the ground under her feet hollowed from the many feet that had come before. At home when she stripped off my clothes for my bath, sand poured from my pockets, sounding like the patter of rain on our wooden floor. I earned those baths.

My brothers came home from the bains-douches smelling of soap and with pink, freshly scrubbed faces. Now we all bathed from the same basin in the same room. We all shivered under a cold washcloth.

Before I'd completed my bath that day, there was a knock at the door from Monsieur Thibou's side and he entered. My mother handed me a towel and I wrapped it around me. My father wiped his hands on a rag, meeting Monsieur Thibou near the door. I watched them speak, and after a brief exchange, Monsieur Thibou left.

"The Kreismans are moving into the apartment across from us," my father announced. Monsieur Kreisman was an upholsterer who'd supervised Severin at Maurice Tsibulsky's shop before we'd gone into hiding. He and his wife, originally from Hungary, had a teenage daughter, Lisa. My parents were not particularly surprised by the news; Monsieur Roger had told us the day before that France was turning on its Hungarian-Jewish population, much as it had already turned on other Eastern European Jews, so the Kreismans were now in as much danger as we were.

Like the Webers, the Kreismans had initially been protected because Hungary was part of the Axis alliance. However, early in the war, Hungary began covertly negotiating an armistice with the United States and the United Kingdom. When Hitler learned of this betrayal, Germany invaded Hungary. Hungarian Jews living in France were no longer protected and they were being swiftly deported to the camps.

The Kreismans moved in later that day. Now another family was hiding near us, another family that had to stay silent at night. During the week, we lived in quiet and deliberate ignorance of each other, but sometimes, on Sundays, Monsieur Kreisman crossed the small landing between our doors to sit with Severin and teach him chess, as Henri and I watched. The pieces were homemade, whittled from discarded wood scraps by Monsieur Kreisman's skilled hands. While he played, he hummed the same song over and over, its melody sad but poignant. One day, after Severin was trounced in a particularly vigorous game, he asked, "What is that song that you are always humming?"

"Kinderyurn. You don't know it?"

"No," said Severin.

His eyebrows raised, Monsieur Kreisman looked at the rest of us. We shook our heads.

"Ah," he said, closing his eyes and leaning back, the crate where he sat squeaking beneath him. "It's a beautiful song. I'll teach you." We sat on the mattress, all in a row like students in a classroom, while he sang the Yiddish song in a clear, strong tenor.

Childhood years, sweet childhood years,
    Always remain alive in my memory.
    When I look back on those years
    I say, what a pity, and pine for those times,
    Oh, how quickly I have grown old.

I can still see my house
    Where I came into the world
    And my cradle, which I see, my friend,
    Standing there in the same place,
    As in a dream, all this has disappeared.

And my mother, how I loved her
    Even though she would whisk me off to cheder.
    I remember every nip of her fingers
    To this very day,
    Even though no trace remains of it at all.

Childhood years like blooming flowers
    Will never return to me,
    Not a sign is left of my house,
    Feigele, too, has left and gone away,
    Oh, how quickly I have grown old.

It was a melancholy song, sung in the eight tones of the Magen Avot scale, a minor scale popular in Jewish music. My mother, scrubbing our linens in a metal bucket, paused to listen to him. Looking back, I think he must have been singing for his own lost childhood, picturing through his closed eyes Hungarian villages with their thatched roof homes, days spent fishing on the banks of the Danube or hiking through the mossy woods - the fern-covered forest floors that German soldiers had recently trampled.

Monsieur Kreisman sang the song again and again that day and, gradually, we learned the words and were able to follow along. Tentatively at first, our voices cracking, then more confidently, until our voices mingled with his into an improvised quartet.

We sang this song about yearning for a lost childhood on many subsequent Sundays. I can't speak to what Severin or Henri were thinking as they sang, but I know that, at ten years old, I did not understand its meaning. It did not resonate that I was experiencing the loss of my own childhood, that I would never be able to indulge in the pleasurable if melancholy nostalgia of Monsieur Kreisman's song. My brothers, too, were missing out on life experiences that would have been happy memories in later years. Severin, 19, and Henri, 17, were young men who should have been entering the world and planning a life beyond the lycée, courting girls in the neighborhood. They should have been sneaking chaste kisses in the dark of a movie theater, emerging love-dazed with tousled hair. Or been out carousing with friends on Saturday nights, dancing until the sky turned gray with dawn, stumbling home with wine-stained lips. Instead, they were leading diminished lives in a cramped warehouse. My brothers had dreamed of adventure, of travel, and just when their world should have been expanding, it contracted. Our carefree years, and those of my brothers, were being stolen. Gone forever.

Also gone forever was the Hungary of Kinderyurn, of Monsieur Kreisman's memory. In March 1944, SS officer Adolf Eichmann was deployed to Hungary to oversee the deportation and murder of Hungary's Jewish population. Eichmann had been present at the Wannsee Conference where the Final Solution was devised; he was subsequently put in charge of organizing the identification and deportation of Jews to the camps. Though Eichmann arrived in Hungary with only a few German staff, the Hungarian authorities were such enthusiastic collaborators that, in just two months, they were able to create over 200 camps and ghettos, which they quickly filled. Eichmann, with help from the eager authorities, was efficient. Between May and July 1944, they saw to it that 437,402 Hungarian Jews were deported, primarily to Auschwitz, where almost all of them were killed.

Though it would be too late for the millions of Jews being murdered in the camps, the tide of war was about to turn. Unbeknownst to us, the Allies were making plans to retake France. Across the English Channel, soldiers were gearing up to run drills on beaches, preparing for the upcoming landing in Normandy. For several years Allied leaders and military planners had been debating the best way to land troops in Northern Europe. By May 1944, more than 1.5 million US soldiers were in Britain ready to participate in or support the cross-Channel invasion code-named Overlord, eventually known as D-Day.

Monsieur Kreisman's chess set survived the war, although over the years the pieces mysteriously vanished, one by one. Perhaps a bishop rolled into a dark corner under a bed, or a knight wandered off in the chubby hand of a squealing toddler, eager to abscond with their prize. Now all that remains of the set is a single well-worn piece, a wooden pawn, and any rough edges are well-burnished by time.

22

SPRING 1944 – A STRANGER IN THE ROOM

I awoke with a start, shocked into consciousness by a foot stepping on me, the heel digging into my chest. My first thought, muddy and unclear as I clawed my way out of a sleepy stupor, was that my brothers were fighting and that, wedged between them, I had accidentally received blows they intended for each other. I pushed myself away, scrambling backward until the dark shape of a stranger came into focus. He was standing over our bed, shouting, his arms waving around. I couldn't understand what he was saying, but his yelling was panicked, piercing, like the wail of an animal in distress. I heard a heavy thud as one of his flailing arms connected with the armoire. He stumbled, almost went down, then bounced off a wall as if he were blind. The thrashing must have lasted only seconds but felt much longer, the time slowed down by my confusion, my brain still sluggish with sleep. Then I understood clearly, and the understanding brought a different kind of fear, razor-sharp and deep: My father was the stranger in our room. It was my father who, more creature than man, was thrashing and bellowing above us.

His hair hung shaggily over his face and his features were distorted, ghoulish. He was shouting in something that resembled Yiddish but was a garbled stew of nonsense words, as if he were speaking in tongues. The moonlight revealed his eyes, wild and white, like an animal caught in a snare. He stumbled about, unseeing, knocking into everything around him – the suspended ham hock, the laundry clothesline. When he collided with his workbench he sent mason jars spinning off and clattering to the floor, where they rolled around us unbroken.

"I need to get out!" That single phrase emerged clearly from the swirling gibberish. "I need to get out of here!" In his blind stumbling, he seemed to be trying to find an exit. My mother launched herself up from the mattress and called to him, dodging his flailing movements as she tried to get close, her nightdress fluttering around her. My brothers and I watched, immobilized by our fear. I looked at my brothers, wanting to be reassured that everything was okay, but they looked just as terrified as I felt. I was not reassured. What *was* this? Not only was Father completely gone, his sightless eyes inhabited by a malevolent spirit, but he was shouting at the top of his lungs, and his screams echoed throughout the courtyard. Papa was breaking our most important rule, which governed everything we did at night: Be silent, be invisible. It was the rule that he'd sternly enforced – with a steely glare, a finger raised to pressed lips – in those early weeks when we were still adjusting to our new life in hiding. It was *his* rule, and now he was breaking it.

Across the hall, the Kreismans huddled together but did not emerge. Later I learned that when Lisa asked her father, "Should we see what's going on?" he shook his head and replied, "No, there is nothing we can do to help them. Stay put." Monsieur Kreisman also whispered reassurances to his increasingly frantic wife but continued to insist they not intervene, even as my father's screams pierced the otherwise silent night, reverberating around the courtyard. The fate of our two families was linked, and if my father's screams brought the police, the Kreismans might be exposed.

I saw Henri and Severin look at each other. We had seen our father lose his temper, which was frightening enough, but we'd never seen anything like this. Father continued to thrash and pace, a caged animal, bellowing as he knocked about our small room. My mother tried to move with him, tried to keep a hand on him while she attempted to reach him with a calm, steady voice, but it was like dancing with an unwilling partner. They lurched around the room in a monstrous waltz, crashing into furniture as he shouted.

A year and a half into our time in hiding, my father had cracked under the pressure of being trapped in this small room, the pressure of living in constant fear for himself and his family. Every time I left the warehouse to buy food, he feared I wouldn't return. That the wrong person would see me as I passed those black-market coupons across the counter. That I would be followed. Each day, he wondered if this would be the day that another German soldier wandered into our courtyard. Or if it would be the day that one of Monsieur Thibou's workers decided he wanted or needed the financial reward of turning us in to the police. The worries were endless and there was no way of knowing when, or even if, this endurance test would end. He had barely survived the horror of Drancy and, having been one of the fortunate few to stagger out alive, he knew more than most what terrors awaited if we were caught. He knew that not all of us would survive. This relentless fear had a vise grip on him, creating invisible fissures until he cracked.

While living in hiding would be hard for anyone, I think it was particularly hard for my father. A walking exclamation point of a man, he was ill-suited to confinement. Before the war my father was infamous within our family for being louder than everyone around him, boisterous even in a subdued crowd, often when my more reserved mother didn't want him to be. More than once, I watched my mother try unsuccessfully to get him to quiet down.

I remember a specific Sunday during one of our regular park excursions, when my father instructed us where to stand for a photo, his booming voice carrying far beyond our family. People looked at us as they walked by, at the three boys in their matching outfits and the loud, well-dressed man who was encouraging them in Yiddish. "Look at my beautiful family!" he seemed to be saying. "Look what I have made!" Standing next to him, my mother tugged on his arm and whispered to him quietly, "Yosel, please speak more softly, there is no reason to be so loud." She saw the people glancing at us and it made her uncomfortable; she wanted to blend in when he wanted to stand out. She shrunk into herself and spoke in a hushed tone, as if trying to occupy less space in the world. But in taking up less room, in using less air, it was as though she'd made more available to him. My father loved to be provocative and he was proud: proud of his boys, proud of his family. Proud of being Jewish at a time when it was decidedly unfashionable, although not yet dangerous. And he responded, still in Yiddish, in an even louder voice, a great smile on his face, "Rikla, my dear, who is shouting?"

Now, my mother was once again trying to quiet my father but with greater desperation. "Yosel, shhhhhh, calm down. You're with us, with your family." She spoke to him as you would to a young child, in a soothing, soft voice, as if she could surround him in a quilt of her words and calm him. "Everything is fine. Sshh now, you need to be quiet. Let's go back to sleep." But he could not be soothed. He continued to shout and bang about the room.

Monsieur Malé heard the noise from across the courtyard. He knocked at our door and Severin bounded up to let him inside. Rushing in, hastily dressed and his hair tousled from sleep, Monsieur Malé quickly took stock of the situation and interlaced his arm with one of my father's while Mama did the same on the other side, boxing him in and walking with him. They paced the room while my mother continued to speak in calming tones.

Gradually, the mad light left his eyes and he became more focused, more himself. He came back to us, spent and exhausted, like a child after a tantrum, his hair slick and his shirt soaked through in large splotches. Reassured that the fit was over, Monsieur Malé left and Mama put my father to bed where he curled up fetal-like, drawing his legs to his chest. We were too rattled to follow right away, the aftereffects of his panic still pinballing within us. Something had broken in our normally steadfast father. Would it happen again? More worryingly, had someone heard? An unfriendly neighbor? A Vichy collaborator? A milicien? Gradually, we slept, or pretended to, each alone in our fear and worry while my father snored next to us.

The morning came and brought a sky that was blanched and heavy, seemingly as fatigued as we were. We acted as if the previous night was a collective dream, something we'd imagined that evaporated in the daylight. Severin crossed the courtyard to go to work in Stairway 9, and Henri and Papa resumed sanding a Louis X cabinet. I circumvented my father like he was something fragile, unsure who he was now. He seemed to have no memory of the night before and behaved as if nothing strange had happened. I don't know if he didn't remember anything or just wanted to forget. We did not speak of it. We never spoke of it. I suppose we all wanted to pretend it never happened. And, of course, there was little space in the warehouse for us to whisper about it without him hearing. But the experience marked us, and the world seemed more precarious than ever. If our father was lost, we were all lost.

One of many Sundays spent in a Paris park, in happier times before the war.
Left to right: Severin, Joseph, Henri. I am in front, looking less than excited.

23

JUNE 6, 1944 – D-DAY

Dot-dot-dot-dash. Tap-tap-tap-Taaaaap. Morse code, the sign of V, for victory. Then the crackle of a man's voice "*Ici Londres! Les Français parlent aux Français ...* [This is London, The French are speaking to the French ...]."

It was hot in the attic. The air had a flat, musty quality, and there was the faint smell of mouse droppings. Henri was concentrating. Perspiration beaded on his forehead and dripped, clouding his vision. He swore softly and paused to wipe the sweat with the back of his arm, then kept twisting the wires of the crystal radio. He had finally succeeded in building it, but it was a delicate, finicky instrument requiring constant tweaking.

The signal was best in the attic, so my brothers and I climbed the wooden ladder from the top floor and crouched amid the attic's debris and dust, cupping the headphones over our ears. Henri was in charge because he'd built the radio, but we each took turns listening. We had a map of France, courtesy of Monsieur Roger, and we marked the Allies' advance using pins. We learned about D-Day and the battle for Normandy on Henri's radio. The Germans forbade listening to the BBC: You were only supposed to listen to German-controlled radio. We'd been told that if a German soldier walked by and heard the sound of the BBC coming out of your apartment, he would shoot at your window, but the Germans could not hear us in our attic hideout, so we listened to the BBC every day. We did not understand the coded messages being sent to the Forces françaises de l'Intérieur (French Forces of the Interior; FFI), but we knew their importance to the war.

The Allies landed on the beaches of Normandy on June 6, 1944. The five beaches where the troops were to come ashore –Utah, Omaha, Gold, Juno, and Sword – were a carefully guarded secret, but, even with the element of surprise, the challenge was daunting. The English Channel was known for spectacularly rough seas and unpredictable weather. Into the water went 1,500 Higgins boats, massive amphibious machines that could deliver troops from sea to shore. Awaiting the Allies when they crossed those choppy waters was the Atlantic Wall: a 3,800 kilometer line of mines, bunkers, and other formidable beach obstacles constructed by the Germans. And at Omaha Beach, the Wehrmacht was entrenched at the top of the cliffs overlooking the landing zone for the American boats. The troops that made it past the Atlantic Wall faced being mowed down by machine-gun fire from above.

Over 4,000 Allied troops died on D-Day, but their sacrifice helped make the mission a huge success. The Allies were on French soil now, and advancing toward us.

Severin and Monsieur Kreisman sat across from each other on wooden crates, the homemade chessboard between them on a third crate. It was July and there was a steady drizzle outside, the first rain in weeks, and the air smelled of petrichor and distant gunfire. "You know," Monsieur Kreisman said thoughtfully, holding a rough-hewn knight over the board as if he were still determining where to place it down, "now that the Americans are here in France, I think it's safer. The Germans are too busy worrying about themselves to worry about us any longer."

My father looked up from his newspaper. "What do you mean?" he asked. There was the hint of a knife's edge in his voice. I was kneeling on the floor, working on yet another wooden block, the incomplete carved B still a P, and I paused. I knew that tone, and I looked at Severin, who knew it, too – if Monsieur Kreisman pressed on, the conversation was unlikely to end well. My father didn't lose his temper often, but when he did, it was terrifying.

I'd never seen my father lose his temper with another adult. It was usually Henri who pushed Papa to a breaking point. Henri was the tinder who could make my father, a dormant bomb, ignite. My irrepressible brother didn't have the sense or restraint to stop before he pushed too far.

One night, when I was still quite young, Henri made my father so mad that he almost overturned the dinner table. I don't remember what Henri was going on about, but whatever it was he wouldn't relent. They went back and forth until my father grew silent and stared at his plate, not looking up at any of us. Suddenly, my father exploded out of his seat. I jerked back, startled.

"Enough!" he shouted, looming over the table and glaring at Henri. He was vibrating with a barely controlled fury. "Enough!" His closed fist hit the table with each syllable, and the plates and silverware bounced with the force of his strike. We jumped with each bang of his fist.

He raised his arm and Henri shrunk back. In one swift movement, my father swept his arm across the top of the table and sent dishes flying into the air, the silverware clanging to the floor. He stormed out of the room.

I remember sitting there in the stunned silence that followed. I was crying quietly and sucking in my breath, scared to move. Henri was also crying. He was trying to pretend he wasn't, but I could see the tear winding down his cheek. Severin glared at Henri. "Why do you always have to stir things up?!" He stood, leaning over Henri. "You need to grow up."

Mama stood as well and started picking up the dishes. She sighed. "Sevek, Henek, stop," she said. "Your father has a lot on his mind and this isn't helping. And Henek, you might try to control that tongue of yours."

She started stacking the dishes. "Boys, help clean this mess," she said, waving her hand in our direction. Limp flecks of cabbage, pale and yellow-green, had been flung everywhere. I plucked a piece from my leg and tried to wipe it on my plate, but it clung to my finger. A small bit of sausage had rolled under the table, leaving an oily sheen as a trail. Severin gathered the shards of Papa's plate, while Henri struggled with strands of cabbage, picking up each piece solemnly. Normally, he would have held a bit under his nose, dangled it like a string of mucus, and pretended to sneeze, or done something else to make us laugh, but he worked with a grim steadfastness, not once looking up.

Monsieur Kreisman had never experienced the full force of my father's temper, but he must have sensed that he was risking it. Even so, he didn't retreat. Not yet. "Well ..." he began, still looking down at the chessboard as if he wasn't sure he wanted to make eye contact. I understood. I had occasionally found myself staring at the ground rather than facing my father's steely gaze. The creases in Monsieur Kreisman's face were pulled tight in a grimace. "I've been thinking that it might be safe to leave the warehouse, to just go back home and live quietly. Mind my own business, lay low." He rolled the chess piece around in his palm. "I think the worst is over. Don't you?" Finally, he looked up and into my father's eyes.

Father folded the newspaper over and set it down with some ceremony. "No," he said, shaking his head back and forth slowly. "I see no reason to think that." He stood and took two quick steps across the small room, placing himself next to Monsieur Kreisman. He seemed to be almost vibrating. There was a furious shimmer around him as he spoke, and I could feel the effort he was expending to keep from exploding. Severin, Henri, my mother, and I, and poor Monsieur Kreisman, we could all feel the undercurrent of fury and watched him in tense anticipation. My mother paused doing her laundry, her hands on the clothesline, on high alert in case she needed to intervene.

"No," Papa said. "Do not say this again. Do not think of it again. If you leave, you endanger *all* of us. And, make no mistake about it, it is *very dangerous* out there." He turned away. "There is nothing more dangerous than a cornered dog," he added firmly, picking the newspaper back up, thus settling the matter. He held up the paper as if reading it, but I think he was using it to cover the storm of anger on his face.

The only sound in the room was the steady drip of water from the laundry on the clothesline, the slow pat of drops hitting the floor. Monsieur Kreisman sighed softly and placed his knight down on the board. "Your move, Severin," he said.

My father was right to be concerned. While the Germans may have been focused on aggressively deporting Jews from Hungary – the highest number of deportations to Auschwitz of the entire war took place between April and August 1944 – the *Milice française* was still active in France and collaborating with the Nazis. Joseph Darnand, de facto head of the French militia, was waging his own war against the French Resistance and the Jews. *La Milice*, known for its brutal methods, was combing through France, deporting or executing anyone they could find. Any pretense of justice or rule of law was abandoned as the miliciens quickly degenerated into roving street gangs, shooting or hanging anyone they wanted on sight. If they were going down, they were determined to bring as many of us as they could find to go down with them.

24

JULY 1944 – THE SCENT OF HOPE

In July 1944, from the small slip of sky visible to us through the warehouse windows, we began to see American B-17 bombers flying in formation toward Germany. I heard the Flying Fortresses before I saw them, the steady rumble of their engines like the purr of a massive feline. In the glare of the sun they resembled yellow crosses, distant stars gliding through the sky. The Germans had an antiaircraft station not far from the Bastille and they would fire at the bombers. The German cannons, known as the flak, could shoot a 20-pound projectile to a height of roughly 7 kilometers. Each time the Germans fired, a siren blared to warn us inside, and then we'd hear the flak making a horrific metallic noise, the sound of the firmament being ripped open. The shells exploded high in the sky above Paris and once in a while managed to hit a B-17, after which the plane would drift out of formation and slowly spiral down, smoke trailing behind like the tail of a lost kite.

The exploded shells rained down throughout the 11th and 12th arrondissements, and often they landed in our courtyard – a hail of twisted metal clattering and bouncing on the cobblestones. When the second, longer siren announced it was safe, dogs howled in the streets, set off by the siren's wail, and I dashed out to collect the shrapnel and stuff my pockets full of it.

In the early days of the war, playing in tall country grass after evacuating Paris with my mother, I'd stuffed my pockets with snails, their calcium carbonate shells curled in fragile beauty. Now, over two years later, I was filling my pockets with different shells, curled bits of iron that were twisted by the violence of war. I held them out in my palms to show my parents when I came back inside. "Do you remember," my mother asked wistfully, holding a piece of the shrapnel between her thumb and forefinger, "how you used to throw coins to the *bal-musette* player?"

I did. The shrapnel that now fell into our courtyard had reminded her of the sound of metal coins landing in the courtyard in a happier, more innocent time. Before the war, 5 rue de Charonne was regularly visited by a bal-musette accordion player, and residents would reward his song with coins. We could hear the accordion's warble through our open courtyard window as the oom-pah-pah of a polka filled the courtyard. I would lean out the window and watch as he rocked back and forth on his heels, his eyes closed as he played. He was an old man, stooped and slight, his shrunken body curled around the accordion. Yet his gnarled hands moved with surprising deftness over the many buttons and keys. I remember skipping over to Mama – *oom-pah-pah, oom-pah-pah!* – and holding my palm out, waiting for her to reach into her dress pocket and take out a couple of coins, which she wrapped in a piece of yesterday's newspaper before handing them to me.

Leaning out the window again, I tossed the wrapped francs; the newspaper made a short arc and then plummeted, landing several feet from the musician. He looked up at me and winked. From other courtyard windows, residents did the same thing. Faces appeared in windows and the packets dropped from above. The newspaper was intended to keep the money from ricocheting off the uneven cobblestones, but sometimes the coins escaped and rebounded with a metallic ding, catching the sunlight as they bounced across the stones.

Residents and workers emerged from their ateliers to have a cigarette and listen to his *musettes,* toes tapping. If there weren't any customers in the charcuterie, Monsieur Meyer would come out his back door and stand, hands resting on his ample, apron-covered belly, while he swayed his head back and forth. René, who always seemed to be outside, weather permitting, might lean on his broom and watch. Even Monsieur Herbin emerged occasionally, arms crossed, the hint of a smile on his face.

When the busker's songs were complete, he shuffled around the courtyard, picking up his coins and then, with a tip of his hat, he would slowly make his way out of our courtyard and on to the next. Heads went back into windows, workers back into their ateliers, and the steady tap of the hammer, the jagged snore of the handsaws, resumed.

On this summer day in 1944 there wasn't an accordion player in sight. But the crash of falling shrapnel, which was the sound of the increasingly desperate German army, was better than any music. According to Monsieur Roger, the soldiers of the Wehrmacht who returned from Normandy looked weary and unkempt; their eyes were haunted, their bearing defeated. In anticipation of a siege, newspapers stopped publishing, radio broadcasting ceased, and restaurants closed. But as Paris prepared for the worst, we started to hope for the best. I dashed around the cobblestone courtyard, snatching up shrapnel and breathing in great gulps of air, air that tasted of gunpowder and metal and smelled like hope.

On August 9, 1944, the Germans started to evacuate from Paris. Ten days later, the French Forces of the Interior (FFI), became active and visible in the city. They took over the Hôtel de Ville – the City Hall – and rode brazenly through the streets with French flags flying from their cars, men sitting astride hoods and leaning from running boards, rifles strapped around their chests.

On August 19, the FFI took over the Préfecture of Police on the Île de la Cité and hoisted the flag of the French Republic, the first time the tricolor had been flown in the capital for over four years. On August 21, in another sign that the war was almost over, the FFI came to rue de Charonne. The French soldiers, assembled from a hodgepodge of Resistance fighters, Communists, Gaullists. and Allied fighters, built a barricade on our street in an effort to impede the German tanks that were patrolling the city. Monsieur Roger appeared at our door, nearly tap-dancing with excitement. "Come! You must come now and see!" he said, beckoning us out of the apartment.

"No, absolutely not," my mother said, arms firmly crossed, when I looked at her hopefully. But Papa, Severin, and Henri went with Monsieur Roger while I was left behind, staring longingly out the window.

My brothers helped the FFI to build the barricade, assembling it from wood scraps and old furniture. Neighbors flooded the street to help, yanking out shipping boxes and damaged cabinetry to contribute, pulling up loose cobblestones and pushing the junk pile together to form a makeshift wall. While they worked to secure it, men from the neighborhood set up a human relay, handing out brass whistles to sound the alert if the Germans came. The owner of the wine shop rolled out a celebratory barrel of wine, but, before he could start passing around glasses, the shriek of a whistle sent out an alarm. The crowd scattered, and my father and brothers bolted back into our courtyard and into the safety of our room.

Monsieur Roger came by again the next day. "When the Germans arrived in their tank, they shot a shell into the barricade to see if it would explode. *Boom!*" Monsieur Roger's hands mimed the outward burst of an explosion. "When they saw it wasn't mined, they plowed right through it.

Like it was paper, like it was nothing at all." He sighed. "Still, one shell less they can use on us, right?" No one was killed, though a neighbor was clipped in the foot by a Nazi bullet as he fled. Days later, limping around with his foot bandaged, he would relate the story of his injury with dramatic intensity, as if he'd been shot while patrolling the forest as a member of the Resistance.

"It's almost over now, Monsieur Parkiet, it's just a matter of time," Monsieur Roger grinned, lifting up his glass of wine as if to toast us. The afternoon sun caught the wine in his glass and it glowed like a ruby in his hand. The excitement was tangible, like an electric current. The air crackled with it. I could hear it in the voices of the tradesmen working outside our window; I could see it in Monsieur Roger. Most importantly, I could see it in my father.

"Do you think we can go home soon, Papa?" Severin asked. My father looked at him with the hint of a smile, a corner of his mouth upturned. I watched the smile grow until it reached his eyes, making them sparkle. It was the sort of smile I'd not seen on my father in a very long time.

"Yes," he said. "Soon."

25

AUGUST 25, 1944 – LIBERATION DAY

We stood outside the door to our apartment, crowded together on the small second-floor landing of Stairway I. It was Friday, August 25, 1944. We had not been in our apartment for over two years. The door was unlocked, but it still bore the dusty remnants of the wax Nazi seal. Moments before, Madame Raymond had knocked on the warehouse door, beaming, her cheeks pink from wine, her eyes glittering with excitement. "It is safe now, Monsieur and Madame Parkiet!" she exclaimed. "We have taken Paris back and the Boche are retreating. Come on, come on!" She waved at us to come out. "You don't need to hide any longer. You can go home again!"

Papa pushed open the door to our old apartment. Even though I knew the Germans had taken our furniture, all the times I'd imagined coming home, I still pictured our apartment exactly as I'd last seen it on the day we fled. My little bed folded and pushed into the corner. Our dining table with its familiar watermarks and scratches. The wardrobe with the cracked mirror. My sailboat. Henri's models. But the door swung open to an empty apartment.

Nothing remained. Nothing. My mother ran her fingers along the place where our wood stove should have been; instead, there was an ugly gash in the wall where it had been ripped out. Even the scuffed linoleum flooring had been scraped away, exposing the dirty, sticky subfloor. When I walked on it, my shoes stuck to the adhesive and the room was filled with a squelching sound as we explored the empty space. We walked around in circles, baffled by the totality of the theft.

Where did our floor go? Why would anyone steal our linoleum floor?

In the corner of the apartment, under the casement windows and wedged behind the gas meter, was a tiny, bright spot of color, a single red flag on a barren moonscape. My father walked over, bent, and picked up the scarlet paper card – it read שנה טובה. Happy New Year. It was something that had been given to us years ago, perhaps at a shop in the Marais. This card was all that remained of our former life. He slipped it into his pocket.

"They took *everything*," Severin said to no one in particular.

My father exhaled. "It does not matter. We are together."

Back in the courtyard we were surrounded by neighbors we'd not seen or spoken to in years. Men clapped each other on the back and women, who'd previously passed each other on the stairs without so much as a greeting, now embraced each other like they were long lost relatives, reluctant to let go. The day workers put down their tools in silent agreement: Labor was done for the day. All of these familiar faces, beaming with joy – the mechanic took a large swig of wine, then handed the bottle to the Italian painter. Even Monsieur Herbin seemed delighted, his face red from happiness, or maybe champagne. Had they known we were in hiding? Were they surprised to see us? I don't actually know. But the moment was larger than us, larger than any one person or family, and the courtyard erupted into a celebration that included us. Madame Raymond enveloped my mother in a hug, almost swallowing her, then released her and disappeared into her apartment, returning with chairs, and wine. Other women from the courtyard, including Madame Nicolas – who had saved us and whom we had not seen since the day she warned us to leave our apartment – brought out chairs, dragging them over the bumpy cobblestones to form a circle. The women sat together, a ring of black dresses, laughing and crying. I stood off to the side and watched them. A brown tabby with a long scar on its nose wandered into the circle, winding itself around the legs of anyone who'd tolerate it. The cat meowed incessantly for milk, and eventually, Madame Raymond's daughter, Paulette, got a saucer and placed it on the ground; today was a day for generosity. Yes, the courtyard took care of its own.

The tricolor unfurled from a few windows, greeted by cheers. Inside the protective walls of our courtyard was the sound of celebration; outside we could hear the sounds of a dying war, the pop of fireworks mingled with gunshots, and the occasional siren. It was the sound of retreating Germans, the sound of a French victory. Smoke plumes rose in the distance, the evidence of ongoing skirmishes in other arrondissements. The day was overcast and foggy, but no one cared. Our courtyard had been converted into a boisterous café, and the wine flowed freely. I looked for Titi, but I did not find her.

Outside the courtyard, the city was even more raucous and joyful. Everywhere were flags of blue, white, and red – mostly the flag of the French Republic, but often accompanied by British and American flags. We heard de Gaulle was in Paris and would parade through the city and attend a service at Notre Dame the next day, August 26. "Rikla, will you come?" my father asked. "I want to see this man with my own eyes." My mother demurred, preferring to stay home, but the next day the rest of us walked toward the great Gothic cathedral. The streets were filled with soldiers in varying shades of olive green, riding on tanks with wildflowers stuck in the crevices, pressed there by grateful Parisians. Young women wore silk flowers of blue, white, and red in their hair and left bright lipstick marks on the stubbly cheeks of beaming soldiers. So much to see after being hidden away for two years and seeing nothing of the world for that entire time! Popping champagne corks were almost indistinguishable from gunfire. Cars with FFI hand-painted in white on their sides drove through the streets, honking and waving, while schoolgirls in skirts and bobby socks crowded for a glimpse of the excitement. I was thrilled to be free, to be celebrating with all of Paris.

The crowds were too dense near Notre Dame, so we stood on the nearby Pont d'Arcole and leaned over the side of the bridge, craning our necks. Men balanced on top of street lamps to get a better view, or perched in trees with spindly limbs that you wouldn't think could hold them. But it seemed like nothing bad could happen on such a day. We saw de Gaulle's car pull up; the crowd surged forward like a single being to watch as he emerged. De Gaulle towered over most men, but with so many people in front of us, I could only see his kepi as it bobbed like a buoy in the great ocean of bodies. The crowd chanted as one *Vive la France! Vive la France! Vive la France!* as he paraded by.

Pop-pop-pop-pop! Shots rang out – the staccato snap of snipers firing down at General de Gaulle! The mass erupted, people shouting and screaming as they bolted for shelter. "Boys, get down!" my father shouted. He pushed my head down and I wedged myself against the cool masonry, trying to make myself as small as possible. I heard the frantic pounding of shoes and the soft thud of bodies colliding with each other as the panicked crowd rushed by us.

"Sevek, Henek, stay down! *Stay down!*" my father said. There was the sound of more gunfire – pop-pop-pop-pop! Pressed down by my father, I couldn't see anything, but I could hear the shouting, the sound of people running, and then the air erupting in even more gunfire as the French fired back and shots rang out from both sides. My father's hand kept pressing, hot and firm on my back, so I couldn't move for what felt like an eternity, though it was probably a couple of minutes at most. Later I read that de Gaulle, even with gunfire raining down around him, continued his unhurried pace through the crowd, tall and unflinching, until he reached Notre Dame and went inside.

The shooting subsided and people stood back up, brushing the dirt and gravel from their clothes. Next to me an older woman straightened the hemline of her green dress and hobbled over to retrieve a shoe, several feet away. Many people had fallen to the ground where they stood, becoming part of a sea of bodies pressed into the street. The air was hazy with smoke from the gunfire. Everyone was rattled, moving slowly toward home. We stood in a semicircle, looking at each other as if seeking validation that what we'd experienced was not a dream. "That was exciting," Papa said, eyebrows raised, his hand trembling slightly as he lit a cigarette. "Let's not tell your mother about that part, shall we?" Severin pushed his glasses back up, and Henri ran a hand through his hair and nodded. If we ever wanted to leave the courtyard again, we'd keep this to ourselves until things settled down.

Back at 5 Rue de Charonne, the celebration had not stopped. Empty champagne bottles were lined against the wall as though being tallied, and courtyard residents were gathered near Stairway 1. Mama, all smiles, was sitting with Madame Raymond and Madame Nicholas in the chairs brought outside the day before.

At the sight of my father, Monsieur Raymond walked over.

"I can tell you this now, Monsieur Parkiet, now that it's safe," Monsieur Raymond said intently.

I stayed several feet away, scanning the ground for bits of shrapnel that I might have missed from recent German bombing.

"You will understand," he said. "I did not want to worry you at the time."

My interest was piqued, and I orbited the adults slowly, still looking at the ground, within earshot but far enough away that they would still speak freely. When you are young it's always best to remain quiet if you want to learn something from adults. They will forget you are there and spill their secrets. And spill he did.

We'd been aware of the milicien who wanted to turn us in but, unbeknownst to us, one of the courtyard's day workers had been trying to get the concierge to turn us in to the police. He came to Monsieur Raymond directly with his proposal. "You know," he said, "there is a Jewish family hiding here. We could make some money if we turned them in to the police."

Monsieur Raymond was an active member of the Communist Party, an ally of the Resistance, and while he was a small man, he could be imposing – at least when he wasn't overshadowed by his wife. He recounted how he'd looked the tradesman directly in the eye. "Listen closely to me," he growled, "you'd better not turn in this family because, if you do, it will be your own family that you'll need to worry about next."

"*Mouches*," Monsieur Raymond almost spat the word, French for houseflies, a term used for informers who collaborated with the Germans. I pictured a man with the eyes of a bug, large and probing, perfect for searching out people in hiding. In my imagination, this mouche had small translucent wings that buzzed constantly and tiny, twitching hands.

"Anyway," Monsieur Raymond finished, "it seems he took my advice, which is all that matters now."

The significance of this information did not register with me at the time. Monsieur Raymond's words landed on my ears like a rubber ball, bouncing away without my understanding their meaning. But the intensity with which he spoke made me remember them years later, and now I do understand. How lucky we were that this mouche made the mistake of confiding in the Raymonds. Luckier still that the Raymonds chose to protect us.

Behind my father I saw Titi emerge from Stairway 3. She was trailing her mother and they were clearly in the middle of a conversation. She was animated, gesturing with her hands. Her brown curls were restrained by a red hairband, her white blouse tucked into a blue skirt. My heart bounded at the sight of her, yet I was transfixed, stuck in place. She looked over and saw me, and I waved at her shyly, a half wave. Titi was taller than me now. She waved back and gave me a small smile. Her face had lost some of the roundness of childhood; there was a hint of cheekbones. For a second, she looked like she might come over to me, but then she ran to catch up with her mother, passing by us and through the arched entrance onto rue de Charonne. My stomach fell. I'd imagined this moment – our reunion – countless times. We'd see each other in the courtyard (as we just had) and Titi would shout – Bernard! – and run over to me, and we'd pick up right where we left off, laughing and playing. In my mind, she was unchanged, the same girl I knew in July 1942. Now I realized that I did not know her anymore. I had frozen her in time, the way it seemed to me we had been frozen, but in the two years that I had been hiding in the warehouse, she'd been attending school, making new friends, and living her life. I didn't know who she was now – she was a stranger to me.

Later that night, small groups of Luftwaffe, acting on Hitler's direct orders, conducted bombing raids throughout the city. General Dietrich von Choltitz, a general in the Wehrmacht and military governor of Paris, had been ordered to destroy the city before the Allies arrived but, whether due to a lack of resources or a desire to preserve the City of Lights (as he later claimed), he defied Hitler's orders. A furious Hitler responded by sending in the remaining Luftwaffe, vestiges of a once mighty Air Force. From the warehouse windows we could see that the sky was a smoky red. The air smelled of burning buildings and my brothers and I jogged across the courtyard to Stairway 9 for a better view. The buildings on the south side of the courtyard were several stories taller than those on the north side; we climbed up to the top floor, to a vacant unit with a small cast iron balcony that faced the Seine. I stood between my two brothers on the balcony and from there we could see fires all over the city. There was one fire larger than all the rest, that looked like nothing I'd ever seen, with flames of greens and blues shooting up through the orange and red.

"Do you think it's going to get much bigger?" I asked.

I must have looked worried. "It's not going to come near us. Look it's on the other side of the Seine," Severin said, pointing to the dark rope of water that bisected the city, separating us from the fire.

"Why is it so many colors?" I asked.

"Don't know, maybe Boches burn differently than the rest of us," Henri said with a shrug. "I'm kidding," he added, seeing my expression.

Across the Seine, in the 5th arrondissement, was the large Halle aux Vins, or wine market. Thousands of casks of wine and cognac were stored there. Later we found out that American soldiers were bivouacked at the Jardin des Plantes, which was adjacent to the Halles aux Vins, and that when the Luftwaffe attempted to strafe their camp, they hit the wine market instead. As the fires intensified, overheated champagne bottles popped, sending corks rocketing. Cognac bottles exploded like bombs, the flaming alcohol producing colors that outshone any sunset. That was what we were watching.

"I can't believe this is over, that we are really free," Severin exhaled. "What do you want to do first? What's the thing you've missed most?" He looked down at me.

I'd missed Titi the most, but now when I thought of her, I had a hollow feeling in my stomach, a kind of sadness that made me unsure. It seemed like she'd changed so much and was no longer interested in me. I didn't want to talk about Titi. I didn't even want to think about her, and I pushed all thoughts of her from my mind.

"See a movie with Papa," I answered instead. Severin nodded.

"Find those *connards* who took my bike and get it back," Henri smiled. "And our radio."

"Ha! I'd like the last two years back," Severin smiled wistfully.

"Me too," Henri acknowledged, nodding slowly.

"Oh! That was a good one," he said, pointing as a large burst of cobalt-blue fire shot up like a rocket amid the orange. It was as though we were watching a fireworks display.

I stood there, nestled between my two older brothers, and I felt safe. We watched as the sky glowed in pinks and purples, with occasional bursts of blue. This last act of a defeated army, this act of destructive violence, was terribly gorgeous. In missing their mark, the Luftwaffe instead put on a light show for all of Paris.

The St-Joseph Courtyard
in the spotlight

5, Rue Charonne, Cour Saint-Joseph, one of the large courtyards so characteristic of the old suburb which smells of wood, varnish and glue. Here is a brave family of Jewish workers, the husband, the wife and the three boys. They were all hidden from July 1942 until the Liberation of Paris, in this very courtyard where they had lived for around fifteen years. It's a neighbor who has provided a shelter room for them. They worked there because their neighbors thought of everything, even getting them a job so they could live. P. is a varnisher by trade and he tells us, "I taught my sons my job, they couldn't go to school, and I assure you, they know how to work now! He is proud of his profession, this Jewish worker.

And how did you get your supplies?

The neighbors helped us, replies the mother, and the little guy, the youngest, came down at the end of every day to take a look at the neighboring shops, the baker, the grocer, the butcher. Everywhere, there was a package prepared for us that we put in our netted bag, all this without the need for words. And the mother wipes her tears while smiling.

So you were under the protection of your French neighbors?

She looks at us.
Sir, she told us — when we went down to the courtyard, the day the Germans were no longer there after two years and a month, we were very happy, weren't we? But our neighbors were crying when they looked at us. And she adds thoughtfully: Yes... two years...

D.D.

134

26

AUGUST 1944 – COKE AND DONUTS

The tents of the American soldiers were the green of ripe olives, and they were spread like a forest of canvas saplings around the buildings of the old menagerie – a zoo that had been abandoned after the French Revolution. The Jardins des Plantes was still closed to the public, but we joined the hundreds of Parisians who gathered outside, faces pressed against the iron bars. In the garden, the Americans strolled with loose-limbed grace, laughing and smoking cigarettes. Sometimes a soldier ambled over to offer a Lucky Strike or Chesterfield cigarette to one of the young women who lined the fences, giggling like groupies. Mostly they kept to themselves. I watched their easygoing swagger; they were like cowboys in crisp military uniforms, tan and fit with open smiles. We stood outside the park, our shabby, threadbare clothing hanging off us, and gawked openly.

Near us, separated only by the iron fence, stood a soldier with dark hair and Semitic features. Papa caught his attention with a wave. "*Amkha* [Member of the tribe]?" The soldier smiled, revealing white-picket-fence teeth, and answered in Yiddish. *Yes.* An invisible bond was formed, a silver rope of commonality that now stretched between us. They chatted through the fence and, before we departed, Papa scribbled our address on a matchbook and passed it through the bars. Dinner. Our apartment. Two nights from now.

Our empty apartment needed furniture, so Papa went about gathering it from friends in the neighborhood. While much was destroyed during the war – dining tables dismantled to build barriers in the street, wardrobes used as firewood, entire apartments looted (like ours) – there was furniture waiting in abandoned apartments throughout the 11th arrondissement. It was furniture decorated by the marks of another life, bearing the fingerprints of previous owners who would never return. Papa had replaced the linoleum floor before we moved back into our apartment and, by the time of the dinner, he managed to collect a dining table and chairs for everybody.

Pvt. Sidney Feldman arrived at our apartment with his hair slicked back and American K rations held forth like flowers on a first date. Over dinner we bombarded him with questions about his life in America and his adventures as a soldier. *Where do you live in America? What's it like? What's your favorite food? Where have you traveled during the war?* He answered our questions willingly, always with a big grin. I don't remember much of what he told us about the war, but I know he didn't tell us everything ("Some things aren't right to talk about over dinner," he said). Thinking back, I am certain of one thing: He saw too much. More than any young man should.

The evening was a great success and Feldman visited several more times, sometimes bringing a few of his Yiddish-speaking friends, always bringing MREs (meals ready to eat). My mother protested his generosity. "Believe me, ma'am, I've had enough of these to last a lifetime. You are more than welcome to them." The packages contained canned meat, hard crackers, chocolate substitutes, and other high-calorie nuggets that were exotic delicacies to our undernourished bodies. Mama made him home-cooked meals of meatloaf and cabbage, which to him must have felt like a taste of home, and he sat at the table chatting with us as she cooked.

Feldman invited me to come to the American commissary. "All the donuts you can eat, and all the Coca-Cola you can drink," he promised. On the walk to the Métro I felt the eyes of the neighborhood on me as I strolled with an American soldier, my personal friend. Maybe it was my imagination but it seemed the other Métro riders also glanced at me with curiosity, perhaps envy, as we rode together, holding the metal pole, swaying with the train's movement. There's no doubt about it, I felt special.

The commissary was bustling, crowded with other soldiers and the occasional guest, mostly young French women. I did not see any other boys like me and I stood proud, with my back straight and tall, as my parents had taught me. The sounds of English buzzed around me, a language I did not yet understand. I was fluent in two languages, but English – less guttural than Yiddish, not as euphonious as French – sounded like neither, landing somewhere in between.

I sat at a metal table, my hands pinned beneath my thighs, my legs swinging with excitement, while Feldman disappeared into the sea of khaki and olive. He returned with a marvelous bounty: In one hand, he carried a plate stacked with glazed donuts, glistening with the sheen of confectioner's sugar; in the other, several bottles of Coke. I'd never had either and watched eagerly as he set them down, the thick green glass clinking on the table. It was like something out of a dream.

Even in the muddiest foxholes on the front lines of the war, American soldiers had Coke and donuts. The American Red Cross trained hundreds of female volunteers – called "donut dollies" – to accompany troops throughout Europe, providing fresh, hot donuts for soldiers who needed a taste of home. The president of Coca-Cola ordered that "every man in uniform gets a bottle of Coke for five cents, wherever he is and whatever it costs the company." The soda company deployed approximately 150 "technical observers," outfitted in army fatigues and commonly known as "Coca-Cola Colonels," to ensure this promise was fulfilled.

I looked at the spread in front of me. "Go ahead," Feldman said, lifting a bottle to his mouth as if to demonstrate. I held the fluted bottle, was pleased by its weight, and took a sip. The fizziness and jolt of sugar delighted me. I guzzled the rest down and followed the soda with one donut, a second, and then a third, the sugary glaze sticking to my cheeks. Feldman smiled as I knocked back another Coke. I had never imagined such things existed, much less gorged on them. My poor, malnourished body did not know what to do with this mad sugar rush. I suddenly felt nauseous and stood at the table, uneasy. "I don't feel very well," I managed before my body jerked forward and everything I'd just eaten splattered onto Feldman's boots.

I was mortified. "I'm sorry. I'm very sorry," I mumbled.

I imagined all of the soldiers were staring at me, wondering who this ill-mannered French boy was. "No, I'm sorry Bernard, this is actually my fault," Feldman said, rubbing my back reassuringly. "I shouldn't have given you so much. I should have known better." He handed me a napkin, his smile so genuine that I knew everything was going to be okay. "Let's get you home."

Me with Private Sidney Feldman, Paris in 1944

27

SEPTEMBER 1944 – A VERY IMPORTANT WOMAN

Like Papa, my brothers and I were eager to walk the streets freely again, so we joined thousands of other Parisians aching to reclaim the City of Lights and slough off the taint of German occupancy. We were excited to move our legs, to stretch the spindly muscles that had atrophied from lack of use. After being locked away for the last two years, every experience beyond the courtyard gates was an adventure. We'd missed the war. It had happened out here without us, and we wanted to celebrate our freedom and reacquaint ourselves with the city.

We strolled across the stone bridges that cross the Seine as it winds its way toward the English Channel, peering down at sailboats that passed beneath us. Wending our way through streets littered with wood scraps and metal grates – the remnants of barricades – we stopped to gaze at the Eiffel Tower like tourists. At the Arc de Triomphe, where de Gaulle had only recently laid a wreath, we stood at the Tomb of the Unknown Soldier, surrounded by mountains of blue, red, and white flowers, overwhelmed by their color and scent. Most of Paris was unscathed, but we did encounter bombed-out buildings and fire-torched homes. Each day we returned sore, with new blisters bubbling, our feet achy and cramped in shoes we'd long outgrown. We loved it. Each time we set out, intrepid explorers, my mother stayed behind. One day turned to another and another until the days turned into a week, yet she'd still not left the courtyard. Not once had she walked through the stone tunnel, past the gates of our courtyard to see rue de Charonne, much less any of the streets beyond it.

"Really?" a stunned Feldman asked when, the next time he came for dinner, we told him. He jammed his hands in his pockets and leaned back in his chair. "Madame, it's a beautiful city. Surely you've missed it!" My mother waved him off. It was not a big thing as her boys got everything for her. She had plenty to do at home.

There was always a reason, always an excuse. But the truth was she was frightened to leave the courtyard. Her world had recently expanded – she regularly visited Madame Raymond and others outside of Stairway 1 – but while the four walls of the courtyard enclosed an area much bigger than the four walls of the warehouse, a prison is a prison, no matter the size. Mama still sent me to run her errands, to get the milk, noodles, and sausage, and she stood waiting for me at the mouth of the arched courtyard entrance, her lips pressed together and her hands clasped tightly in front of her until I came back.

The next day, Sidney returned with three friends, American soldiers wearing identical khaki uniforms and matching broad smiles. Sidney offered my mother his right arm. "Madame Parkiet, it is safe now. Come with us. We promise we won't let anything happen to you. It's time to see Paris again." She took it tentatively, trembling.

The soldiers encircled her and gently moved her forward, the way you might corral a skittish horse. She balked, she demurred, she shook her head, but they were persistent. Finally, she took a step forward, cautiously, as if she feared the ground beneath her might crumble, or rise up and to devour her.

Only decades later did I fully understand how terrified my mother must have been. For over two years she had remained in one small room, leaving only to empty the chamber pot in the toilet half a flight up. My brothers and I made occasional trips into the courtyard for work or food; we'd each, however briefly, had the opportunity to breathe air that hadn't already been inhaled by other family members. Mama had only a narrow space that smelled of varnish and sweat. The small size was claustrophobic but also reassuring: You could take the measure of it. Those four walls had protected us, but that didn't mean she felt safe. She didn't complain, and she didn't break down, but for two years she brined in worry, attuned to everything. *What was that sound? What is going on outside? Are they coming for us?* She marinated in that ever-present fear until it distilled into a dark smoke snake that wound through her veins. It had been her constant companion, and she could not let it go.

The soldiers walked her through the arched tunnel and emerged onto rue de Charonne. My father, brothers, and I, eager to be there for the momentous occasion, followed and observed as they paused, allowing her to take in the thrumming street, teeming with life. *Deep breath.* The Americans conferred in English, our mother almost invisible in the center of them, a bud of a blue dress peeking out. Then Sidney nodded his head to the right and they moved toward rue du Faubourg Saint-Antoine. The sun was out from behind the clouds and there was the tickle of a breeze; it stirred the French and Allied flags dangling from windows and they briefly swayed in the air, as if waving to us. I stayed several paces behind, walking next to my father. At the corner, a car backfired, a loud pop like the sound of gunfire. Mama startled, and if the Americans had not held onto her arms, she would have bolted back toward us. "It's okay, Madame Parkiet," they said. "It's just a car. You are safe." They continued again. Two girls, arm in arm and looking smart in flowered dresses, shared a bemused smile as they passed. They weren't the only curious ones. Almost everyone smiled at our unusual procession. *Who is this petite, unassuming woman and why does she need a military escort?*

We turned right on rue du Faubourg Saint-Antoine, heading toward the Bastille. With each step, Mama shed some of her fear; she stood taller and walked more confidently. We marched forward with increasing enthusiasm, a tiny, exclusive parade of nine. In front of us, two men in coveralls moved a dresser off a handcart. They paused to nod at the soldiers and smile at my mother. She smiled back widely. A bell jingled as the door of a boulangerie opened, emitting a puff of warm yeasty air, of something sweet. A man in a beret with a tricolor armband, laughing and smoking, leaning against the building, called out after us: "Who are you escorting, Americans?"

"A very important woman," one of the soldiers called back in schoolboy French.

Now that we could see that she was enjoying herself we began to as well, basking in her excitement at seeing the city once again. We were all smiles, talking and pointing. *Look, the movie theater is still there.* A few more steps and we were in front of the photography studio. *Remember when we got our photo taken? Looks like he's still in business, too.* Inside the studio, the same moon-faced man was adjusting the height of his tripod, while in front of him posed a young couple. Next, we passed the cobbler. *Look, Mama, your favorite shoe shop is still here.* The shop appeared open but with a depleted inventory. Before the war, she liked to pause in front of the window to take in the selection of dress shoes with shiny buckles or tassels – the cherry-red heels and the Oxfords in robin's egg blue. Though she rarely purchased anything, she loved to look. Now, a mousy woman arranged a small selection of plain, practical shoes in the window. We passed the art deco sign for the Métro and the street opened up to the large circular plaza of the Bastille, traffic spinning around it like bees around a buzzing hive. Cafés lined the Place de la Bastille, the tables filled with people enjoying the mild weather. *Look. Now it's American soldiers at the tables instead of Germans. That's a welcome sight!* We stopped and watched the life around us. A flock of strutting pigeons, necks as opalescent as an oil slick, pecked at something on the ground. A man on a bicycle went by in a streak, splashing up water from the gutter. The pigeons scattered briefly then settled, necks jutting and bobbing again. A blur of cars shot off in different directions from the traffic circle. And everywhere – on armbands and as lapel pins, on lampposts and from windows, even draped on the column at the center of the Bastille – was the flag of the French Republic.

The Colonne de Juillet, or July Column, is a bronze commemorative pillar standing in the very heart of the Place de Bastille. We stood there, my family and I, surrounded by our strapping American escorts, gazing up at the great column. Originally envisioned as a monument to the first French Revolution, it was eventually built to commemorate another: the July Revolution of 1830. At the very top of the 52-meter-tall column, poised on a large gilded globe, stands a golden, winged figure, the Génie de la Liberté (Spirit of Freedom). Leaning forward on one foot in an almost balletic movement, the figure extends a torch – the torch of civilization – in his right hand. In his left, he holds the remains of the broken chain of bondage. The figure celebrates the freedom of the French people.

We remained there for some time, my family and our American friends, taking in the vibrant, pulsing heart of the Bastille. *Our city is still here.* Only a month before I'd watched from a window as the Americans in their B-17 Flying Fortresses thundered past on their way to Germany. From our small room, which was both refuge and prison for over two years, I watched the cross-shaped planes in the sky and felt hope. Now, these four Americans were my mother's own Flying Fortresses: They swooped down and gave her back her wings. On this day we stood on the former site of a massive stone prison, a prison that was destroyed on July 14, 1789, in order to make way for the first French Republic. It was there, at the Place de la Bastille, a location symbolizing independence and liberty for all of France, that my mother once again became free. The American soldiers liberated France, and then they liberated my mother.

28

AN EMPTIER CITY

The first time I saw the dead body of someone I knew, it was in a photograph. Uncle Israel was shot in the street when soldiers caught him selling cigarettes illegally sometime between 1942 and 1944. My warm, gregarious uncle, who would ruffle my hair with a grin whenever I passed him, who was the life of every party. He died where he fell, crumpled in the middle of a cobblestone road in Lyon, surrounded by a crowd of silent onlookers and a pool of his own crimson blood. No one objected to his execution. No one moved to lay a coat over him as he bled to death in the street. The police took a photo of his corpse before hauling it off to be burned, as was the practice with so-called traitors to the Vichy regime. Witnesses stood by passively, not wanting to meet the same fate.

"They shot him like a dog, like he wasn't a person," said Aunt Sabine, her eyes brimmed with furious tears.

In the weeks after liberation, French citizens who had fled south in 1940 started trickling back into Paris. Our aunt returned from Lyon with Micheline and Huguette. They reclaimed their apartment on rue de Crussol, emptied of all of their stylish furniture, the polished floors scuffed beyond recognition by the shoes of strangers. Each carried only a leather suitcase secured with brown twine, all that remained of their possessions. Pressed between the pages of a book, as one might preserve a wildflower, was a picture of Uncle Israel's dead body. A gendarme gave Aunt Sabine the photo, perhaps so she could identify his body, perhaps to serve as a warning to her and to their friends.

I remember the odd thrill of fear, the surprised jolt when I saw the picture of Uncle Israel. I leaned close, disbelieving, until my aunt slammed the book shut and put it away. In the photo, my uncle looks surprised, his eyes wide open, as if startled both by his violent fate and by what had happened to his adopted home of France.

In autumn 1944, when the days had grown chilly and short, Pvt. Sidney Feldman received notice that his battalion would be shipping east to join the Allied advance toward Germany. France had been liberated, but in much of the rest of Europe, the war raged on. He came to say goodbye and to return his key to our apartment, which Papa had given him earlier as an indication of our regard and as encouragement to visit. He started to put the key on our table, but Father waved him off.

"Keep it," Papa said. "You are always welcome here and, when you return, you will need it." While it was largely a symbolic gesture, it conveyed an important message: Sidney was now a part of our family.

"Okay, I will," Sidney said with his easy smile. "Now I can tell my friends that I've got a home in the US and one in Paris. Very fancy." His smile faded briefly. "Though I don't know when I'll be back; we are heading toward Belgium and, with luck, into Germany. We've got the Führer on the defensive now, and we have to keep moving."

My mother's lips pursed in a familiar expression of concern and she cocked her head to the side. On top of worrying about us and her missing family members, now she had an American soldier to worry about as well. She had grown fond of Sidney for his warmth and sense of humor.

"Now you know you are part of the family," my father joked, noticing my mother's face, "Rikla's worried about you." He clapped Sidney on the back. "She's not wrong to be. Please take care of yourself. You are our favorite American soldier, and we want you coming home to your family in New York and to us, your French family."

"Also," Papa said, pulling him aside, "if you happen to be in Brussels, will you try to stop by this address to see if Rikla's sister is still there?" He handed over a piece of paper with the address of Aunt Maryla and Uncle Romek. Brussels had been liberated, but we had not heard from our aunt and uncle and Mama was concerned. "If they are safe and well, you may get a home-cooked meal out of it."

Sidney was correct: Hitler was on the defensive and increasingly vulnerable. After landing on the coast of Normandy, Allied forces continued inland, moving eastward toward Germany, while, in Eastern Europe, the Soviets advanced westward. Germany was sandwiched between these two advancing armies, at risk of being completely surrounded.

Despite how vulnerable the Germans were, Hitler had one last surprise. Believing he could repeat the success of the 1940 Ardennes initiative, he pushed for a similar offensive now. Germany needed to halt the Allies' Western advance, and Hitler thought that if he could break through their advancing battalions, creating a hole in their line, he might also rupture what he believed was a fragile alliance between Britain and the United States.

My parents were right to be worried. Sidney and his battalion were heading off to fight in what would be the largest and bloodiest battle of World War II – the Battle of the Bulge. Starting December 16, 1944, German guns pounded the Allied line. It was a frigid December, with temperatures hovering around 20 degrees Fahrenheit. Stormy, cloudy skies kept US planes grounded, hampering the Allied advance. German troops pushed forward through the tangles of the Ardennes Forest, creating a bulge in the Allied lines that gave the battle its name. If the Germans had breached the line, things might have ended differently, but they failed. The bad weather broke, the Allied planes took to the air, Britain and the United States pressed forward, the bulge flattened, and the Germans finally retreated. After the Battle of the Bulge, Germany's surrender was a foregone conclusion.

A couple of months later, we received some desperately awaited news. Aunt Maryla wrote, confirming she and Uncle Romek had survived. "They're fine! All of them!" my mother yelled, waving the letter. "Oh, what a relief." She wore a huge smile, as huge as the weight that had been lifted. "And listen to this!"

She chuckled as she read: "Well, it seems that you've been keeping some fine company! Imagine my surprise when several American soldiers showed up at my door, saying you sent them. I was grateful to hear that you are all safe and sound. We, too, have survived intact." Mama got such a laugh out of thinking of Sidney and his friends showing up in their uniforms. How surprised her sister must have been.

"Can you just imagine! Oh, if I could have seen her face when the Americans explained." She shook her head and grinned.

Rationing was still in place in France post-liberation, and it would be several years before food supplies returned to prewar levels. Lack of food stunted my growth, cheating me out of much of my adolescent growth spurt. I was malnourished, with scrawny arms and visible ribs. So my father took me to a farm in Lucenay, outside of Lyon, where food was more plentiful. I stayed for a couple of weeks, drinking milk still warm from the cow and eating freshly killed chickens. I spent my days running through tall grasses with Tulip, a big Beauceron farm dog who herded the cows to the barn each night. Another boy my age lived there and I helped him – quite inexpertly – with some farm work, lugging tawny bales of hay and pails of water. My Christian hosts tended to me as if I were one of their crops, feeding me and giving me plenty of sunlight. At night, with the unfamiliar trill of crickets in the air, I lay under a thick cotton quilt in a small room with a wooden crucifix on the wall. I stared at the mournful visage of Jesus, sculpted in oak. I'd never seen a cross before and it intrigued and unnerved me. Jesus was thinner than me but not as emaciated as the camp survivors who would soon begin to trickle back into our neighborhood.

29

THE RECKONING

The horrors of the camps in Eastern Europe were unknown to us in those early months. While government leaders had access to more information – Allied leaders learned of death camps as early as 1942 – knowledge in our community was spread through word of mouth or the slow, erratic delivery of letters. There was no way to get real information, only rumors. To this day, it's not clear to me when the adults around me understood the scale of the massacres, when words like "genocide" and "Holocaust" began to be used. Looking back, I'm sure my parents were far more worried about our family in Poland than they ever let on. We never heard them speak of their fears. After liberation, Mama sent letters that either disappeared unanswered into an abyss or were returned as undeliverable. My parents must have known things were bad, yet there was no way to know how bad. I'm sure they hoped that their parents, siblings, and young nieces and nephews were hiding in attics or sequestered in a rural village. That, wherever they were, they'd been protected by others, just as we had. But they were not so lucky.

I'm not even sure when *I* understood what had happened in the camps. I was a child who until recently had been afraid of the dark, of monsters that lurked in dark corners of stairways and basements. I didn't understand that real monsters thrive in the dark corners of a corrupted heart. I don't remember being told, but at some point I just knew. It was an awareness that came as gradually as a breaking day. The black of night hides the truth of everything and we are left to the roughness of our imaginations. Then the sun starts to rise beyond the horizon and, by degrees, the emerging light of day reveals the texture of the world, the truth of it. Things that once seemed scary may be revealed as harmless: A large black shape might be a fallen tree. But the bright of day also reveals atrocities previously hidden by the night. The large black shape might not be a fallen tree after all but a pile of broken bodies, murdered and left to rot. Suddenly the light is blinding, unsparing, illuminating everything. When that happens, it's almost impossible to remember that, only an hour or so before, you didn't know the truth. Some horrors, once revealed, seem to become part of your DNA.

Even before we knew the truth, it was obvious that people were missing: The neighborhood had been culled and felt emptier. It wasn't just Jews who were missing, of course, but also young men who had been conscripted to work in factories far away or gone off to fight for France and never returned. But the missing Jews were many. The shop of my father's friend Maurice Tsibulsky, where Severin had apprenticed in the early days of the war, remained closed. Papa walked by once a week, peering through the dark windows. He knocked on nearby doors, inquiring after his old friend. Had anyone seen him? His wife or children? In return, he received only shaking heads.

When Father returned to work in his old workshop at Stairway 9, dusting off his workbench and refilling the mason jars that had waited for him for over two years, the door to the workshop across the landing also stayed closed. Old Monsieur Sherapan, whose gnarled hands had fascinated me with their surprising skill, was gone. He had lived with his family in the adjoining courtyard, Cour Jacques-Viguès, and their apartment was empty.

"Yes, they came for them the day they came for you," Madame Raymond acknowledged sadly.

It was the Kreismans who told us that Monsieur and Madame Weber were missing. The couple who had taken me to the Marne River for a picnic, who had treated me to my first taste of túrós csusza and given me a rare opportunity to bask in the sunlight and inhale the fresh scent of green grass, had been arrested and deported to Auschwitz once Germany ended its alliance with Hungary. That was the fate the Kreismans had avoided thanks to Monsieur Thibou. The burly, mustachioed Monsieur Grósz, business partner of Monsieur Thibou, had vanished, too, presumably for the same reason. And of course Monsieur Adler had died even before we went into hiding. We were surrounded by the ghosts of our former neighbors. There were so many missing that the accounting was overwhelming.

In the spring of 1945, survivors started arriving back in Paris from the camps, shuffling back into the city, skeletons in striped pajamas. As they arrived to be processed in Gare du Nord, de Gaulle quickly realized that the survivors were far too sick to be sent on their way without medical care. To house them, he turned over to the Red Cross the Hotel Lutetia, a luxury hotel on the Left Bank where he had honeymooned with his wife. The 233 rooms of the hotel were now hosting the shell shocked and malnourished victims of the camps. Photos from that time show emaciated survivors, still in their striped uniforms, in a luxe dining room, eating bread and drinking water out of fancy silver cups, their bodies too deprived to handle rich foods. Crowds waited outside the hotel, searching the gaunt, unrecognizable faces of the survivors as they walked by, looking for their families or friends. They posted flyers with old photos of their missing loved ones, asking survivors if they'd seen their father, their daughter, their sister.

Months and months passed for us with no news of missing friends and family, including from Poland. Finally, Madame Tsibulsky and her daughter Anna visited us, bringing the horrific news of what happened to them. The Tsibulsky family had been deported to Auschwitz. Father and son had died in the camp. Knowing now what inmates endured – the backbreaking labor, capricious slaughter, starvation, disease-ridden conditions, and harsh winters – it's amazing that mother and daughter survived. It's amazing that anyone did.

I remember two teenage girls about my brothers' age who lived on the same street as Aunt Sabine; they returned from Auschwitz with sharp cheekbones and a solemn, faraway look in their eyes. Before the war, they'd had a little brother my age, but he died in the camp, leaving them with a ragged, bottomless hole in their heart. In me, they saw echoes of their lost brother. They doted on me, bringing treats – pale nougats in colorful metal tins – and hugging me. They squeezed me as if to remember what it felt like to hug their little brother, the imprint of his body on theirs.

In January, the Soviets launched a winter offensive, driving westward. They advanced on Berlin, and the fate of Germany was sealed. On April 30, 1945, Hitler, hunkered down in an underground bunker, swallowed a cyanide capsule and shot himself in the head. On May 1, German radio, not wanting to reveal that their leader had committed suicide, instead announced that Hitler had fallen fighting Bolshevism.

On May 7, Germany surrendered, and though I have no specific memory of how the news was received at 5 rue de Charonne, I imagine there were whoops of delight and expletive-filled toasts to the Soviets with glasses held high. While my parents closely tracked the news of the day, reading the newspapers and listening on our newly purchased radio, the more pressing concern was still basic survival: getting enough work to put food on the table (Father) and finding food to purchase amid the rationing still in effect (Mother). Any celebrations in our house would have been brief, followed by my parents going right back to rebuilding our lives. I had more immediate concerns myself; I was back in school, working hard to catch up after missing two years.

That August, my family returned to the beaches of Berck-Plage, the coastal town where we had vacationed each summer before the war. Berck-Plage is about 300 kilometers north of Paris on the Opal Coast, an area of northern France that got its name because of its soft, opal-like light. The beaches are distinguished by fine sand and rolling dunes, tufted grasses that sprout in large plumes. Before the war, the coast of Berck-Plage had been kilometers of unspoiled beach, broken up only by wooden huts and the occasional restaurant. But during the war the coast had been defiled by Germany's massive Atlantic Wall – the concrete fortifications designed to protect Europe's west coast from an Allied assault – and the area sustained additional damage during the Allied invasion.

Madame Raymond and Paulette came to Berck-Plage with us, and we rented a small clapboard house a short distance from the water. None of us could swim but we waded in the shallow waters and watched the tiny minnows, like flashes of silver, that darted around our feet. We had picnics under beach umbrellas and I raced my brothers on the hard-packed sand, dodging waves. We watched the tide fill in the impressions left by our footprints.

All around us were reminders of the war. Remnants of concrete bunkers were slowly being consumed by the fine sand and we climbed on the ruins like playground equipment. The beach was dotted by a number of defused naval mines – gigantic metal globes that sat on the sand, dark and forbidding. Germany deployed thousands of these floating contact mines during the war, where they bobbed harmlessly in the ocean until a ship bumped into one of their contact spikes, detonating it. In subsequent years, unexploded mines would continue to wash ashore periodically and bomb-defusing teams would be called to do the dangerous work of removing the detonator, extracting the cylinders of explosive that filled the belly of the mine, piling it on the sand, and lighting it, where it burned like a sparkler.

We took turns clambering on one of the marooned explosives. There are several photos of us posing on it in our swimsuits. In one photo I'm leaning against the defused mine and my left palm rests casually on one of its spiky triggers, now neutered. Severin is perched atop the globe, his right arm slung around my shoulder, and Paulette sits next to him. The adults stand behind and slightly to the side of us and the sun is on our faces as we squint at Henri, who is taking the picture.

I can remember the heat emanating from the metal orb as it sat in the sand like a black star covered in graffiti scrawls, the heat warming my body where I pressed against it. Somehow, we had outlasted this dense metal monster. Somehow, our soft, fragile bodies had survived the war intact while this mine had been gutted. Once it could have brought down a warship, but now it was just a giant metal ball soaking in the sun's heat and sharing it with us.

Posing on defused naval mine on the beaches of Berck-Plage, 1945. From left to right: me, Severin, Joseph, Paulette Raymond, Madame Raymond, Rilka

30

THE PURGE

The purge, or *épuration sauvage*, began shortly after liberation. Both formally and informally, collaborators were prosecuted for their crimes. In some regions, citizens took it upon themselves to impart justice, holding public hangings in the town square. Horizontal collaborators – women rumored to have been romantically entangled with a German – had their heads forcibly shaved before being paraded barefoot through the town, enduring the taunts of neighbors.

More formally, the government rooted out Vichy sympathizers for prosecution in the *épuration légale* – the purge trials. In our courtyard, the authorities cast a suspicious eye on the Meyer family, originally from the German-dominated region of Alsace-Lorraine. Surely, the Meyers, with their Germanic roots, had aided the Nazis. Surely, they'd rooted for them. Surely, they at least had Vichy sympathies.

"They don't believe me!" Monsieur Meyer exclaimed, in a mixture of frustration and fear. We ran into him in the courtyard as we were picking up our mail. *Je ne suis pas un collaborateur* [I am not a collaborator]!

"They know nothing about me. They are only looking at where I was born, and they don't see anything else." He was waving a letter from the government. "I'm all for punishing Vichy collaborators, but this ..." he shook his head, genuinely baffled, "this is ridiculous. They are demanding proof of my innocence. Perhaps, Monsieur Parkiet, perhaps if you explain that we *knew* you were in hiding, that we not only didn't turn you in but kept food aside for you, for your family. Perhaps that will persuade them of my innocence."

"Of course." Father nodded enthusiastically. "It would make me happy to be able to help you and your family after all you've done." He provided a formal attestation to Monsieur Meyer's character, and the inquiry was dropped. The courtyard took care of its own. And for once, Papa was on the giving rather than the receiving end of that care, which must have been gratifying to him.

In 1946 Henri enrolled in the prestigious École Boulle, studying in the newly launched interior architecture program. A bit of art and science blended together, interior architecture is the reconstruction and reimagining of interior spaces. Henri had planned to continue refinishing furniture, to master the trade he had begun learning during the war, but Papa recognized that he actually yearned for something else. The boy who had spent his childhood making models would be the first in our family to get a secondary education. He and Papa hauled a drafting table up our spiral staircase and pushed it against my parents' bedroom wall between the two casement windows looking over rue de Charonne. Henri worked at it each evening and, provided I was quiet, I was permitted to stand near him and marvel at the art nouveau buildings that he brought to life on paper, the beautiful filigree detail that his ink-stained hands created.

I was in high school now, after a rigorous year where I worked to catch up with what I'd missed during the war. My father, who'd not been able to attend school himself, wanted to make sure that I took advantage of the opportunity. Each gray morning, with the sky spread like a blank canvas above me, I walked a route to the Lycée Charlemagne that took me past the July Column and its triumphant angel, past the art deco movie theater that I regarded possessively as belonging to my father and me. At the intersection of rue Jean Beausire and rue de la Bastille, I passed the women who clustered at the corner, smoking cigarettes, a flock of brightly decorated birds. The prostitutes greeted me each day – *Bonjour chéri!* – as I strolled by; it was a friendly greeting, with no hint of lasciviousness, and I always responded "Bonjour" with a wave in return. Each of us was just starting our day, doing the work that life had assigned to us, getting by in a country still picking itself up from the ground, emerging both triumphant and tarnished from the war.

Father was back in his workshop and business was good. Both Severin and Monsieur Kreisman resumed work at the Tsibulsky family upholstery business, taking on more responsibility in an effort to fill the hole left by the deaths of Maurice and Jan. Titi and I encountered each other in the courtyard sometimes, and we'd nod and then go about our business. The hollow, pitted sensation I'd felt upon realizing our friendship was over had subsided into a dull ache. Life moved on, but France felt different. The tricolor still swung from windows and flagpoles in celebration, but for my parents and their remaining friends, there was no denying that many Parisians had stood by while Jews were rounded up. As she stood in line at the Marché d'Aligre, how could my mother not wonder if the woman in front of her was quietly disappointed that Vichy France had been defeated? As he sat on the Métro, how could my father not wonder if the stoic face across from him had supported the Nazi efforts to murder all the Jews of Europe? We may have been protected, but others had not, and now the shine had worn off our country. Maybe that's why, after years of casual consideration around the dinner table, we began to seriously discuss the possibility of a move to Palestine.

It wasn't the first time Father raised the idea: He'd also proposed it in 1935. He'd felt the tug of an idea, like the nibble of a fish on a line. Back then, Mama was reluctant to move. Palestine meant a rougher life, and the 1930s in particular were marked by pogroms and infighting. My brothers were thriving in Paris, and I was still toddling around in diapers. In the three years she had lived in France, my mother had already come to love it. After some deliberation they decided to stay in Paris, but the idea of a move never left my father's mind.

Israel was established on May 14, 1948, and the British, who had ruled the region for 30 years, promptly departed, rolling their tanks and sand-colored jeeps into large ships and leaving behind empty barracks and miles of coiled barbed-wire fencing. Immigration became more of a possibility.

We weren't the only ones considering a move. Paulette Raymond had already departed for the United States as a newlywed after a whirlwind courtship with a barrel-chested American soldier. The Kreismans also relocated to the United States, finding a new home in Detroit, the bustling hub of the growing US automobile industry. And while René still sold music boxes from an atelier in the courtyard, Monsieur and Madame Raymond were talking about retirement, which would mean leaving 5 rue de Charonne. I could sense my father considering a move to Israel, weighing the idea over, examining it from all sides. It became a regular dinnertime discussion.

One night he asked us directly, 'What do you boys think: Do you want to move to Israel?" He glanced at Mama. This was clearly a conversation they had been having for some time. She nodded and rose to put on the tea kettle. Rain had started outside; it was tapping at the windows and the apartment felt cozy.

I thought about it seriously in the silence that followed. Something about the idea appealed to me. I'd been watching Palestine, now Israel, on the newsreels that played before movies, and I don't know if something about them reminded me of the cowboy movies I used to love or if it was just the prospect of adventure, but the idea of moving there excited me.

"I think we should go," Severin said.

"I agree." Henri nodded.

I watched as my mother set down a cup of tea for my father and the steam danced. Papa's head tilted, and he smiled at them and nodded. "Okay, but you should know there is a war going on there." Arabs and Jews had been fighting for years in Palestine, but after the withdrawal of British troops, the fighting escalated. On May 15, 1948, the First Arab-Israeli War broke out immediately after the announcement of the independent state of Israel, with Arab forces invading from several surrounding countries.

Father stirred sugar in his tea, the spoon dinging against the teacup, and looked at us expectantly.

"If everyone uses the war as an excuse, no one will go," I responded, sitting up in my chair and looking directly into his eyes.

Father rewarded me with a small smile, his eyes twinkling. I could tell I'd pleased him, and I felt a rush of pride. There was no one I wanted to impress more than my father.

"Not to mention," Severin added, "that France is fighting a war too. We're probably going to have to fight either way." Severin straightened his thick black glasses and cleared his throat. "I'd rather fight for Israel."

"Yes, me too," Henri agreed.

In 1948, France was struggling to maintain control over Vietnam, its colony, in what was then known as the Indochina War. De Gaulle, now president of France, believed firmly in the need to keep France's empire strong. The French colonies had formed the initial kernel of de Gaulle's Free French forces when he was building his government-in-exile from London, and he was reluctant to let them go. While there was no active conscription, the government had threatened it as a possibility if the conflict persisted, and both Henri and Severin could be drafted if that happened.

With that conversation, the idea of immigrating started to take shape. It became something on the horizon, something tangible and within reach, and we moved toward it.

In the spring of 1949, at the southern port city of Marseille, we joined hundreds of other Jewish immigrants waiting to make *aliyah* by moving to Israel. It seems odd now, but I don't remember leaving our apartment and courtyard for the last time. I don't remember what it felt like to leave the only home I'd ever known. I was 15, incapable of nostalgia and excited about the adventure, propelled toward the future I would create. I don't remember saying goodbye to our neighbors. I'm sure that Madame Raymond would have enveloped my mother in a hug, my mother's narrow shoulders disappearing into Madame Raymond's broad ones, but I don't remember it. I'm sure that I didn't say goodbye to Titi since I hadn't spoken to her in years.

I do remember that, in preparation for the move, we sold our furniture and almost everything we owned, packing only essential items into suitcases. Under Henri's arm he carried an oil painting he'd made during his time at École Boulle, one of the few items he'd selected to bring along. Carefully wrapped in a protective sheath of cardboard, it was a painting of Monsieur Thibou's warehouse when we lived there – a painting of our hiding place, without us in it.

Henri's painting is from the vantage point of someone standing at the foot of our two twin mattresses, near the door to Thibou's workshop. In the upper left corner is the door to Stairway 6. To the right is the wardrobe that held the few clothes we had, and our chamber pot peeks out from behind it. The mirrored front of the wardrobe is reflecting the room. At the top of the painting is the laundry line, strung from one wall to another across a corner, clean linens dangling to dry, stiff with a sort of rigor mortis until we used them and brought them back to life. Below the hanging laundry sits the wicker chair, and on the chair is our box of meager foodstuffs, elevated to protect against the mice that scrambled in the dark. Light streams into the room from the unseen windows to the left of the painting, illuminating the low wooden table in the middle of the room, the table where we gathered cross-legged on the floor for meals and whispered conversation. On the right side, Henri has painted the small cast-iron stove, and on a burner is the tea kettle, robin's egg blue, that we snuck back to retrieve in the early days of hiding. Even the ham hock hangs from the ceiling, waiting for one of us to carve off a slice. It's the room exactly as it was when we lived in it.

For over two years we hid from the Nazis, from our country, in that warehouse. Every family conversation, every interaction was conducted in that one sparsely furnished room. It's where we worked, ate, read, sang, fought, slept. Looking at that painting, it's clear that, on August 25, 1944, before we left that room forever, Henri paused to look back. Before we went down to the courtyard as a family, before we joined our celebrating neighbors and reclaimed our apartment, rejoining our old lives, Henri stopped and scanned the room one last time, taking a mental photograph of what he saw so he could paint it later.

Henri Parkiet's painting of the warehouse belonging to Monsieur Thibou during the time the Parkiet family was in hiding there (July 1942-August 1944).

31

1949 – ISRAEL

It was March 1949, and we were bouncing down the unpaved roads of Haifa in a bus that rattled like it would soon crack open. In our wake was a trail of diminishing dust contrails, and the air coming through the open windows was hot and humid, bringing no relief. I felt limp with the heaviness of the atmosphere, and my head lolled around lethargically as I rested my neck on the back of the seat.

We'd just finished a week on a ship, the old *Theodor Herzl*. Hundreds of us were making the journey, and we all slept together in one large open room on metal bunk beds lined up as in a military dormitory, chained to the ceilings so they would not move in turbulent waters. The boat, one of several large passenger ships named after the noted father of Zionism, was chartered by the Jewish Agency, which covered all costs associated with our immigration. It was one of the last voyages for the *Herzl*. Built in 1907, her coal-fed engine was starting to fail, and her metal-plated sides were covered in rusted scrapes that looked like old bloodstains. She would be sold in 1950 and scrapped by 1952.

Once we arrived in Israel, we were put on the bus and, as it left Haifa behind, I stared out the window at the long stretches of undeveloped plains and rolling hills covered in scrubby, hardy-looking bushes and cacti. The road was lined with white rocks that looked like broken teeth. It was like the landscape of a different planet. Everyone was weary from the long rough boat trip and tempers were short. We were sweaty and gummy, our skin sticking to the unyielding wooden bench seats. A black fly buzzed around our heads, further heightening the irritation. Time passed slowly, and the landscape gradually changed; patches of wildflowers sprung up between bottlebrush trees. Another hour and the land showed signs of agricultural development; we passed miles of unfamiliar trees, in rows like soldiers. Two hours into the trip, the bus driver, a small, dark whippet of a man, pulled over to the side of the road. "Be right back," he called out with a baffling level of enthusiasm and he leapt off the bus, seemingly unbothered by the heat that had put the rest of us in a torpor. We watched apathetically as he disappeared into a row of trees, and moments later he emerged from the greenery with armfuls of oranges for everyone. "Have a taste of Israel, of your new home," he said, walking down the center aisle of the bus and passing out the fruit. The oranges filled the bus with their perfume, and soon everyone had forgotten the dust and their fatigue. We were smiling and laughing again, the juice all over our faces and hands, making us stickier still. My father told the story of the bowl of oranges he had put on a table in Paris to welcome my brothers. It seemed like a good omen, the beginning of yet another new life.

The oranges were our second gift of the day: Only hours before we'd been bestowed with Israeli names at Sha'ar Ha'aliyah, the immigration processing center. Hundreds of immigrants stood in a swaying clump there; our bodies, having finally synced with the rhythm of the sea, were at odds with the stillness of the land. We waited in a long queue, lumpy with suitcases and the occasional piece of furniture, while the sun hammered down on us. It seemed like a new, different star from the one we knew in Paris; this sun was virile and aggressive with something to prove. By the end of the day, our faces would be red and sun-slapped.

At the front of the queue, a man in a linen suit sat behind a table. "*Shalom!*" he greeted us, his right-hand hovering over a giant ledger. "Name?" With the mark of a pen, my father Josek (Yosel) became Yosef. Mother (Rikla) became Rykla. Severin (born Sevek) again became Issahar. Henri (born Henek) became Chaim. I had been born Binem, lived the first 15 years of my life in France as Bernard, and now, standing in front of the Israeli immigration officer, I became Benjamin. New names ... the unasked for, and often unwelcome, gift of immigration. Hebrew names, because we were Israeli now. We nodded, accepted these new names with a smile, and then kept using our old ones.

Our next stop was Be'er Ya'akov, a tent village in a former British army camp. Our family got our own tent – dun-colored canvas raised over the hard-packed dirt. The tent was equipped with a military camping stove, a gas lamp, and five separate metal beds with loose, well-used bedsprings and thin cotton mattresses.

"It's not fancy, but at least we have our own beds," my father said, turning around in the tent. "We have certainly survived worse."

"As long as I don't have to share a single bed with you two again," Severin said, nodding at me and Henri, "I'm happy."

In the camp we began group classes to learn Hebrew, the language of Israel. My father had assumed we would speak Yiddish in Israel; it was the language he'd grown up speaking, the spoken language of the Eastern European Jews. We were surprised to arrive to a national campaign – "Only Hebrew" – designed to enforce a single language. People were immigrating from all over the world, and a common language was considered necessary to create a national identity. Everywhere we went, billboards were promoting the "Only Hebrew" movement, but my father was unfazed. "Hebrew? *Shmegegge*. I didn't come all this way just to be told I can't speak Yiddish," he said.

There was a massive decline in the use of Yiddish following World War II. The vast majority of Jews targeted by the Nazis were Yiddish speakers, and many Yiddish-speaking survivors emigrated to new countries, where they learned the local language in order to assimilate.

I don't know exactly when or how my parents learned that their family in Poland had not survived. There were informal channels – people placed ads in the newspaper looking for family members – and there were more formal ones. Through the International Tracing Service, the Red Cross took on the mandate of tracing victims of Nazi persecution, documenting their fate, and making the information available to survivors. However they found out, my parents never shared it with me, and like many survivors, they kept this pain largely to themselves.

After several months in the tents, we were moved to the Baracks, cinderblock ex-military housing that had been organized into areas of common nationality and language. Along with other settlers from France, we now lived with hundreds of immigrants from France's many colonies. I made friends with an amber-eyed girl named Rachel, whose family had come from Turkey. I taught her to ride a bike, running behind her with my hand on the back of the seat as she pedaled furiously along the winding paths of the camp, her jet-black hair flowing behind her. Several years later, she would marry Severin.

That winter our family was transferred to low-income housing, a small apartment southeast of Tel Aviv in the suburb of Giv'at Rambam. Compared to the Spartan accommodations of the refugee camp, this newly built apartment was luxurious: There was electricity and gas, a small kitchen, and a bathroom. "A kitchen! Our own bathroom!" exclaimed my mother, her hands pressed together. Shortly after we moved Severin and Henri left for the army, and it was only my parents and me in the apartment. I attended high school in the nearby city of Tel Aviv where modern buildings rose, white and gleaming, out of the shimmering desert. I entered the mathematical and engineering track out of a sense of what I wanted to do next. Like Henri, I felt the pull toward architecture, but while he had concentrated on the construction of buildings' interiors, I wanted to focus on the buildings themselves. I'm not sure why it called to me: Maybe I was inspired by the beautiful buildings of Paris, or maybe it was the new, glistening Tel Aviv. Maybe it was from watching Henri work at his drafting table. Going even further back, maybe the seed was planted back in 1937 on that magical day when we walked around Paris and gaped up at the buildings of the World's Fair. And, while I wasn't yet sure how, I thought I might want to study in America.

32

1957 – AMERICA

On December 31, 1957, on the cusp of a new year, I boarded a ship for the United States. It was only my second boat trip – the other time having been the passage to Israel – and the trip to the United States was comparatively luxurious. I'd finished high school in Tel Aviv and served several unremarkable years in the Israeli military, and now, at age 24, I was heading to California where I was going to study architecture at the College of San Mateo, a small community college in a sleepy hillside town south of San Francisco.

Our ship would dock in New York, where I was to visit my great Uncle Charles. Charles Parket (he, too, had lost the "i" in Parkiet, not at birth but when he immigrated to the United States before World War II) lived in Brooklyn and owned a cleaning-products store on Lexington Avenue in Manhattan. I'd never met him, but he had provided an affidavit of support, an essential component of my student visa application. The affidavit was a promise to provide me with financial support since I wasn't supposed to work while I was in school. While I had every intention of getting a job, I felt the US embassy didn't need to know that. When the embassy official told me that Uncle Charles's salary wasn't enough to cover my expenses, I had to get a second affidavit. This one came from the Kreismans, who were still living in Detroit.

It was raining when I arrived in New York, a sharp rain that bordered on sleet. I'd caught a cold during the journey and by the time I disembarked I was feverish and exhausted. Uncle Charles waited at the bottom of the gangplank, a small man waving enthusiastically from underneath an umbrella. He was accompanied by two of his daughters, crowded under a second umbrella, their cheeks a splotchy pink from the cold. "Welcome to New York!" he bellowed, pressing me into the wet woolen folds of his coat, the sleeves slick like a seal's coat from the sleet. "We have thrown a party in your honor!" he proclaimed, squeezing me so tight I thought my ribs would crack. It seemed he had adopted the over-the-top American enthusiasm I'd heard so much about.

Oh, no, I thought, but what I managed to say was: "Ah, thank you very much," though I think my delivery was less enthusiastic than both of us would have hoped.

"You've had a long journey," he acknowledged, thumping me on the back so I almost pitched forward. "But this is exactly what you need." He looked at me for a moment, taking in my pallor, the grayish hue of my face, and then he nodded so enthusiastically that it seemed he was nodding for me, too. "Family! Friends! And some good American food!"

I stumbled around the reception, woozy and semi-delusional, bouncing from one guest to another like a slow-motion pinball, shaking hands and trying to be gracious. I don't remember much of it and afterward fell into a deep, dreamless sleep in my uncle's guest room, surrounded by boxes of the borax and castile soda that he used to concoct his cleaning products. I spent several days sweating and shivering in bed before the fever broke. I remember a doctor visiting, the cool of the stethoscope on my chest, some white tablets, and water to wash them down.

Throughout the years, I'd kept in touch with Sidney Feldman. We started writing letters after the war, corresponding in English, which I'd studied in France and Israel. I had written to him that I was coming to the United States via New York and, since he still lived in Long Island, we made plans to get together.

He arrived at my uncle's right from work, wearing his navy-blue police uniform. I remember being excited and a bit nervous, my stomach jittery. It had been 13 years since I'd last seen him and I wondered if it would be awkward. When I first met him, I was a skinny, pale kid, 11 years old, underfed and overwhelmed. He was a young soldier, fighting in a worldwide war. To me, he'd been a superhero. I don't recall clearly, but the first moment

I opened the door might have been awkward as we reconciled our memories with the reality in front of us. This version of Feldman was older with a rounder, softer face. But then his wide grin opened up, familiar and warm, and time evaporated.

Sidney rubbed his eyes in mock disbelief. "My God, Bernard, you are a grown man," he said, shaking his head and laughing." I don't know why I expected to find a boy. It's so good to see you, you look very well!" The spell was broken and we came together and embraced.

He sat at my uncle's table and I brought out bottles of Coca-Cola, extending the familiar glass bottle to him. "For old time's sake," I said, adding, "I promise not to throw up on your shoes this time."

Sidney erupted in a guffaw. He was the sort of person who laughed with his whole body, his head thrown back as if the laugh came over him in a wave and he just rode it. "Much appreciated," he said, still chuckling at the memory. "I'd completely forgotten about that." He held his bottle of Coke up. "L'chaim [To life]! To old friends and fond memories."

After his tour of duty, Sidney entered the police academy and was now a sergeant in New York City. He was married, with three children – a boy, a girl, and now a baby boy – and they had a house on Long Island. "Paris sure seems a long time ago," he said. "And a couple of pounds ago, too," he added, looking down and patting his soft stomach ruefully. He slapped the table with his palm and leaned toward me. "And you! You must be about the age that I was when I met you and your family."

I smiled at that thought. "That's probably true," I agreed. I picked at the paper label on the Coke bottle as I pictured myself back in the American commissary, my legs swinging from the chair as I watched him come toward me with a plate of stacked donuts. "It's hard to imagine, but it's probably true. I'm glad that I'm heading to school and not heading off to war."

"I'm glad as well," he said, nodding slowly. My old friend was rarely serious, but he looked somber now. "You may not have been a soldier in the war, but what you and your family survived was a different kind of war. Let's hope we don't live to see anything like it again." Outside, mingled with the background noise of traffic, I heard the sound of children playing in the street, the shouting and laughing that accompanies a game, and I thought about all those days I spent locked up in the warehouse, all those days I listened to the other kids playing in the courtyard and wished desperately that I could join them.

"I'll drink to that," I agreed, and we raised our Coke bottles in a toast.

Uncle Charles took me to the airport for the next part of my journey – a flight to California, with a short layover in Detroit. He pressed $50 into my palm and hugged me before sending me on my way. It was my first time on a plane, and I marveled at the bright interior, the rose-red carpet, the poppy-orange seats. Takeoff was loud, something I hadn't expected, and I remember the feeling of being pressed down into my seat by an invisible hand and the rattling of the overhead compartments. I looked out the window and saw the Earth falling away, the city of New York becoming a miniature model of itself below me.

In Detroit, the Kreismans met me at the gate, shouting my name as I stepped off the plane: "Bernard! Bernard!" Like Sidney, they were familiar but changed. Mr. Kreisman's dark curly hair was gone, replaced by a horseshoe of gray that went around his otherwise bald head. Mrs. Kreisman, in a sheath dress and navy heels, was put together and elegant in a way that I'd never seen her before. Their daughter Lisa also had a new air of glamour, her dark curls cut stylishly short, her lips painted the color of ripe strawberries. I had a couple of hours until my next flight, so we found a corner of the terminal, tucked away from the briskly moving travelers. We sat on brown vinyl chairs, leaning toward each other and speaking quickly, trying to cram as much in as possible while, through a crackling loudspeaker, a disembodied voice announced which flights were departing next. The Kreismans ran a successful upholstery business in downtown Detroit and lived in a three-floor brick townhouse that they owned. They had a Chevy sedan, canary yellow. America had been good to them.

"Here we are together on the other side of the world. We are so very lucky," Mrs. Kreisman said, shaking her head at the wonder of it.

Were my parents happy in Israel? *Yes, very, happy, as long as you don't make them speak Hebrew.* Severin? Still playing chess? *Happily married with two young children, so not a lot of time for chess these days.* Henri? *Settled and happy, but don't worry, still managing to cause trouble.*

The loudspeaker announced that my plane was boarding soon and Mrs. Kreisman thrust a parchment-wrapped roast beef sandwich into my hands. "So that you aren't hungry on the plane," she said, and I saw that her eyes were welling with tears.

"Thank you," I replied, looking at the sandwich in my hand, moved by the motherly care it symbolized. I was also touched that they had come to the airport to see me. "And thank you again for the affidavit of support. I don't know what I would have done without it, without you. You really saved me there."

"Nonsense," Mr. Kreisman said, waving the idea away. "It was our pleasure. The least we could do."

"Your father ..." he said, and I heard the hitch of emotion in his voice. He paused and cleared his throat before continuing. "I owe your father my life. My family's lives. I ... well, I was sick of hiding in that room and I wanted to leave. He wouldn't let me, and he was right. It wasn't safe." He finished by wrapping his arms around me and slapping me on the back. Then Lisa hugged me, kissing my cheek and leaving a smudge of strawberry. Finally, Mrs. Kreisman embraced me, squeezing me before releasing me. "As much as we want more time with you, we don't want you to miss your plane, dear. You'd better go."

In California, the college had arranged room and board with a family in San Mateo, and in return, I helped out with household chores. After a couple of years, I transferred to Stanford University on scholarship, living briefly on campus before moving into an apartment with other Israeli students. To make sure neither my uncle nor the Kreismans would need to make good on their affidavits of support, I worked as a bellman at the Benjamin Franklin Hotel, a 99-room luxury hotel. Part of my salary was in meals, and during the quiet hours, I was able to study, parked under the goose lamp at the bellman's desk, reading textbooks and eating the strawberry shortcake that accompanied my dinner.

I thought I had it all worked out. I was almost done with my degree and soon would head back to Israel where, as an architect, I would help to build the future of my new country. I would design more gleaming buildings that would rise out of the desert. Everything was going according to plan. And then I met Orah.

33

1960 – FOUR DATES

My roommate Amnon loved to throw a party, and on this September evening in 1960, he invited all of the Israelis we knew. The apartment was packed, Elvis Presley was spinning on the turntable, and I was sitting on the carpet chatting with a friend when I saw Orah standing in our kitchen, coltish and shy. She looked unsure where to go and which group to join, so I beckoned to her and patted an empty spot on the carpet beside me. She came over and sat down, her legs folded under her like a pocketknife. When she tilted her head toward me, her auburn hair hung like a curtain, framing one side of her face.

I'd met Orah once before, about a month earlier, at her birthday party in San Francisco. Amnon and I had given her and her friends a ride home from the celebration, and I remembered the way she paused as she got out of the car and looked back at me expectantly, as if she was waiting for me to say something.

Orah is a Sabra, a native Israeli born before her country. When she was 15, her father became entranced by the idea of moving to America. Orah's older sister, Channa, stayed in Israel, but the rest of the family immigrated to San Francisco, settling in the fog of the Outer Sunset district in one of the candy-colored rowhouses lined up like chiclets along the neatly drawn streets.

"Do you miss Israel?" I asked. I missed it. I loved California but still wanted to return to Israel as soon as I finished college.

"Yes," she said, picking at the tufts of our avocado-green carpet, there were some things she still missed: her friends, the weather, the calm of the

Mediterranean Sea. There were other things she didn't miss: dirt roads and dogs snapping at her feet when she rode her bicycle.

Someone turned up the music. With each passing hour, the party got a bit louder. A cup was knocked over, with a laugh and a shout. Dancing feet pressed potato chips into the carpet. I grabbed a bowl of pretzels from the kitchen counter, sticky with spilled drinks and crumbs, and placed it between us. We took turns asking each other questions and while answering hers, I fed her pretzels one by one, trying to seem sophisticated. Finally, at about 3 a.m., Orah's friend called to her. It was time to go home.

Seven hours later, I picked her up for our first date.

On our fourth date, as we sat in my car overlooking the vastness of the Pacific Ocean, I proposed. Less than a year later, on June 25, 1961, we were married by a rabbi on the ground floor of the Tulip Room on Geary Boulevard, the sort of nondescript event space equally suited for a birthday party or bingo. My groomsmen and I wore matching white jackets, boxy and midthigh length, with black trousers. The bride, of course, wore white.

While I was surrounded by friends, my family was back in Israel and I missed them. I made a phone appointment via an international operator to speak with everyone on the morning of the wedding. Everyone had gathered at Henri and his wife Stella's house in Tel Aviv to celebrate my wedding. Even Orah's sister, Channa, and her husband, Moshe, were there. The operator connected me and my parents answered together, sharing the receiver. Behind them, I could hear the sound of a rowdy party and could picture my parents cradling the phone between them. Meanwhile, Henri popped a bottle of champagne to the sound of cheers. I held a microphone to the receiver and recorded the conversation: the voices of my parents and the celebration around them. I could hear the joy in their voices, and I choked up. They were on the other side of the world.

My mother wanted to speak to Orah.

"Mama, Orah doesn't speak either Yiddish or French. She does speak Hebrew."

"Ah, Hebrew. That's not going to help." Like my father, my mother had steadfastly refused to learn Hebrew.

"She also speaks a bit of German."

"Maybe she will understand some Yiddish then?" my father suggested.

There were five languages between our two families, yet we could not seem to find a common one.

"Well, Orah's father, Joe, is from Poland originally and he speaks Yiddish," I said.

"Finally! Someone who speaks the real language of the Jews. Put *him* on the phone."

So Orah and I watched, her hand in mine, as our Polish fathers, both named Joseph, happily chatted via a copper submarine cable that stretched around the globe. They had never set eyes on each other but were united by a country of origin, the language of Yiddish, and, most importantly, the love they bore their two soon-to-be-married children.

34

SUMMER 1962 – FAMILY

A year after our wedding, we made the trip back to Israel so I could introduce Orah to my family. My parents still lived in Giv'at Rambam in the same apartment we'd shared when we first arrived in the country. Severin and his wife Rachel lived in Lydda, a suburb just south of the airport, with their two children, Tsipi, age seven, and Roni, three. He was working as a bookkeeper at a large export company. "I love my work," he said, shrugging and smiling. "It's logical. There is always a right answer." I had a memory of him sitting at the dining table in Paris, helping my father with his invoices, writing carefully in the glow of a gas lamp. He'd always been good with numbers.

By contrast, Henri and Stella lived the life of bon vivants in Tel Aviv. He had his own practice as an interior architect, and his studio was attached to their apartment. Early in the marriage they'd tried for children but, after a while, they put that dream aside and moved on to another, embracing the artistic lifestyle. Their friends were painters and musicians, and Henri liked to entertain, throwing exuberant parties. Stella was a sculptor, creating abstract figures that, twisting and rising out of metal, always seemed to be grasping at something just out of reach.

Henri and Stella had everyone over for dinner, and we squeezed around the dining table before spilling into the living room. Our numbers had grown and our happiness could not be contained. After dinner, Henri put on a record and we danced in the living room, waltzing in couples. I took a turn around the room with my mother before stepping back to watch my parents dance together. Standing between my brothers, I savored the scene: our wives, all three wearing flowered dresses and white high heels as though they had coordinated in advance, were laughing in the kitchen. My parents swayed, their heads together as they slowly turned in circles. All of the people I loved were gathered together in one place. Father's back was still strong and straight, his eyes retained their twinkle, and though he'd thickened around the waist, he seemed healthy. My mother had settled happily into her matronly years, potato-shaped and smiling. The watchful, careful expression that I remembered from my youth had softened and she had seemingly relaxed into accepting the happiness that was her due.

"They look good," I said to Severin. "How's their Hebrew?"

"Ha!" He rolled his eyes and laughed. "Their French is better."

My parents never would learn Hebrew, and that was just fine by them. They had a quiet life and kept largely to themselves. As in Paris, in Israel they had a small circle of Yiddish-speaking friends – Holocaust survivors and European refugees.

As the night wound down, my father waved enthusiastically to my brothers and me to join him in front of the fireplace with my mother. "Come on, come on. You know where to stand. Stella, will you do the honors?"

It was time for us to reenact the family photo from June 1942 when we had marched down rue due Faubourg Saint-Antoine to the photography studio, bright yellow stars sewn into our formal black clothes. The reenactment had become a family tradition on the increasingly rare times we were all together. We had last taken one five years earlier, right before I departed for the United States. For that 1957 portrait, we went to a studio in Tel Aviv and, dressed in black and staring somberly at the camera, we posed in a manner similar to the original. Of course, in the 1957 photo, we were not wearing the yellow stars.

The photo from the summer of 1962, taken in Henri's living room 20 years after the original, was less formal. The men were in white button-downs, sleeves rolled up, and Mama wore a dress with a bold, geometric print. We were flush from dancing, smiles on our faces, standing in front of the brick fireplace. After taking the photo, we squeezed together for another that included our wives. My brothers and I squatted in front, each with one knee on the carpet, while Stella, Orah, and Rachel stood behind us. My parents took their regular positions, standing on either end like bookends.

All too quickly, the visit was over, and Orah and I went back to California. A couple of years later, we were delighted to welcome our first child, David. He was serious, sensitive, and watchful. Four years later, in 1968, a girl followed, Karen. Giggly and dimpled, she was quick to smile and equally quick to lose her temper. Four years after that, in 1973, another boy arrived, Michael – a grinning terror who lunged at the world and who made us look at each other and decide, right then, that we had enough children. And not enough space for them in our small home.

In 1974, we purchased a house that didn't exist yet, a four-bedroom being built as part of a small development in Palo Alto in an area surrounded by fruit orchards. We watched the house go up before our eyes, parking our wood-paneled station wagon across the street and eating turkey sandwiches in the car, gazing at the construction like it was a drive-in movie, our kids squabbling in the back seat.

Every couple of years, we visited Israel, sometimes stopping in Paris on the way so I could visit my courtyard. Walking on those familiar cobblestones, I would soak in the memories and absorb the changes since my last visit – the cars and trucks that replaced horse-drawn carriages, the new mustard-yellow shop signs that jutted out from the ground floor of the buildings. In Israel, I saw the passage of time on my parents with each visit. The lines on their faces were deeper, and they moved across the room more slowly. Maybe there was a slight hand tremor or a wobbliness in the walk. A curve to the shoulders, a stooped back. When you don't see someone often, aging seems to happen faster.

Yet even as my parents grew old, as their steps slowed into shuffling, they seemed very much themselves. My mother still cocked her head to the side and, hand on her hip, smiled at me in a way that told me she knew what I was thinking. My father's eyes still had a sparkle, his wit was intact and, to me, he a remained powerful figure. That is why it was startling to me that when Orah and I visited in the summer of 1978, while my mother was fine, something seemed different about him. Every once in a while I would see a faraway look in his eyes, like a shadow falling over him, and the spark momentarily dimmed. It was disorienting. His mind had always been the quickest of all of ours, and now it seemed to falter at times, like an engine that stalled unpredictably.

"What's going on with Papa?" I asked Severin.

Severin's lips puckered as if he had tasted something sour. He frowned. "I wasn't sure you would notice. Sometimes he gets confused. Or he forgets where he's put something, like his wallet. It's sporadic, and it seems worse at night. It's not bad, at least not yet, but if it gets worse, I don't think Mama is going to be able to care for him."

I felt an ache in my chest at this news, a slow burn of sadness that spread outward from my heart. I knew rationally, as everyone knows, that my parents wouldn't live forever. But it's the sort of knowledge that lives in the brain, not the heart. The physical distance between us made this even harder.

Even more alarmingly, Henri also looked unwell. His face was tight, he'd lost some weight and it seemed to me that he barely ate.

"I keep telling him he needs to go to the doctor," Stella said when she saw that I noticed his lack of appetite.

Henri waved her off. "You are making too much of this. I probably have an ulcer like Papa had." For months he had suffered from bouts of indigestion and heartburn and, remembering how Father had struggled to manage his ulcer, he assumed he was dealing with the same thing.

"Well, we'd know for sure if you'd just go to the doctor," Stella said, tamping out her cigarette with an angry flourish and turning toward me. Her eyes were two dark coals, smoldering. "It bothers him more than he's saying now. He's as stubborn as a mule, as you know well."

Henri sighed. This was clearly not the first time they'd had this conversation. "I'm over 50," he said. "I can't eat like I used to, even if I wish I could. That's all the doctor's going to tell me."

It seemed possible, even likely, that Henri was right. But no matter what he tried, his symptoms never improved. So weeks later, long after I had returned to California, he gave in to Stella's urging and went to see his doctor.

"Stomach cancer," he said when he called me on the phone, "Stage four."

Suddenly it felt like the air had been sucked from the room, like I was in the empty abyss of space, floating, adrift. I put my hand on the wall to steady myself.

"Look." He paused. In the background I could hear the sound of dishes being stacked, of Stella in the kitchen talking to someone. I pictured Henri standing at the door to his living room, the cradle of the wall-mounted phone wedged between his shoulder and ear. "Now that I know what it is, at least I can work on treating it."

"Also," he said, and I listened to his footsteps as he crossed the tile floor, moving away from the noise of the kitchen, "the doctors here seem to know their stuff, but I know that fancy school you went to has a top-notch medical facility. Can you see if they are doing anything new there? Anything I should know about?" The background noise had faded and I pictured the phone cord stretched out as far as it would go, no longer curly, now taut and tense. "Anything that might help me?"

I called Stanford. I spoke to everyone I could. The message was consistent. *The doctors in Israel are just as good as what we have here. They are some of the best.* And that was true. It was also another way of saying a different truth: There was nothing I could do. There was nothing anyone could do.

1957 family portrait, in Israel. From left to right: Rikla, me, Henri,
Severin, Joseph.

Visit to Israel, 1962. Left to right: Rikla, me, Henri, Severin, Joseph

Visiting Israel in 1962. Standing, from left to right:
Rikla, Stella, Orah, Rachel, Joseph. Crouching, left
to right: Henri, me, Severin.

35

1979–1989 – FAREWELL

In early 1979, I was selected to join a team overseeing the development of two air bases south of Tel Aviv in the Negev Desert, a project that emerged from the 1978 Camp David Accords. For 13 days in September, at the rustic presidential retreat in Maryland, President Jimmy Carter facilitated negotiations between Egyptian President Anwar Sadat and Israeli Prime Minister Menachem Begin resulting in a historic peace accord. One of the concessions Begin made was to return a swath of land on the Sinai Peninsula. As a consequence, Israel relinquished two air bases it had constructed there, and the United States committed to help Israel build two new ones in the Negev.

Being selected for this project was a significant professional opportunity for me, one that was too good to pass up. And since the enterprise required us to relocate to Israel for several years, it meant being able to spend time with family. Orah would be near Channa, and I was grateful to be able to spend more time with Henri and see how he was weathering the chemo and radiation. When we spoke on the phone he tended to minimize the seriousness of his situation, but I was worried. I also wanted to spend more time with my father. Over the previous year he'd grown increasingly ill, and now he was too frail for my mother to tend to him, so he was living in a care facility outside of Tel Aviv.

I flew to Israel in May of 1979 for a month of preparatory work on the airbase project. The days were long and I often found that by the time I glanced at my watch it was after the sun had set. Had I eaten lunch? Or even breakfast? Who knew. Despite the long days I made sure to squeeze in visits with family. Henri had lost weight, and he clearly had bouts of pain, but he was generally in good spirts, and remained optimistic.

Several times a week I slipped away from work in order to visit my father in the assisted living home, a muted building with soft tones and carpeted hallways where the smell of Aqua Velva hung heavy in the somnolent hallways. Everyone there seemed drowsy and sluggish, as though they existed in limbo between life and death. Walkers were lined up against the walls, waiting to be reclaimed, and in various alcoves the residents dozed in their wheelchairs, mouths slack.

My habit was to sit with my father in the late afternoon, keeping him company as his nurse, a round, sturdy woman named Sarah, performed her regular checks. She delivered pills of different colors that rattled around in a small Dixie cup and he begrudgingly took them one by one, a ritual that seemed to move in slow motion. She lifted his arm gently, wrapping it in a cuff to take his blood pressure, squeezing the balloon to inflate it until it looked like it would cut off his circulation.

"She's the best, isn't she?" Papa asked. "Make sure to give her a good tip, Binem." Sarah and I smiled at each other as she wrapped the blood pressure kit back up, putting it back in its blue vinyl bag. When she entered the room, it was glowing orange with the late afternoon sun, and by the time she finished her checks, it was a cool blue with twilight.

In June I visited my father on the way to the airport. My advance work was done and I was heading back home to prepare for the move, scheduled for August. I told my father I'd be back in a couple of months with Orah and the kids. I watched Sarah as her hand, soft with youth, moved his shrunken, spotted arm into the blood pressure cuff – an arm that in its sinewy prime had lifted me with ease and was now discolored with deep purple bruises from being poked and prodded. I chattered on, telling my father how excited I was to introduce my kids to Israel and that they were anxious and didn't want to leave California. But I thought they'd love it, I said, and I was grateful they'd have more time with him and the rest of the family. Maybe they'd love it so much that we'd decide to stay and build a new life here. Papa nodded, but I wasn't sure how much of what I said was sticking. These days, my father seemed to live either in the distant past or the immediate present. Still nodding, he looked at Sarah and turned back to me. He smiled.

"Binem, this nurse, she works hard. Make sure she gets a good tip," he said with a wink.

"I will Papa, I will." I took his right hand and felt the familiar nub of his shortened index finger; my hand closed around the stump instinctively. I remembered walking down rue du Faubourg Saint-Antoine and clutching his knuckle – back when my head barely came up to his waist, when I had to take two strides to match his one – as we headed to the movies on a Wednesday evening. I remembered how special I felt being with him, sharing something that was only for the two of us. I knew I had to leave for the airport, but I sat there holding his hand for just a moment more. His skin was gradually turning crepey, almost translucent, as if he were literally disappearing in front of us, as though if we turned away for a moment and then looked back, he might be gone.

And then, one day, he was. I got the phone call from Severin. My father passed away on Tuesday, July 31, only days before we boarded the plane to return to Israel.

I suppose that all children start off adoring their fathers, whether or not that adoration has been earned. My father earned it, time and time again. How many people can say their father saved their lives? Proud, but never boastful. Quick to anger, quicker to laugh. A jester, a teaser. A provocateur. The only thing he loved more than a good argument was resolving one, bringing peace between quarreling people. Once I saw him resolve an argument between two strangers who did not share a common language – one who spoke only Yiddish and another who spoke only French. He stepped between them, acting as translator and bridge, solving their quarrel. He was someone who could always find a path forward – a dealmaker, but not at the price of integrity. Typical of many immigrants, my father always seemed to be looking toward the future and he rarely wanted to dwell in, or even discuss, the past. But I wish now that I had talked to him about what we all went through together in Paris during the war. We left so much unsaid.

In preparation for our return to Israel, Orah packed two large suitcases full of Cheerios, the bright yellow cereal boxes stacked in rows, the blue Samsonites bulging but disarmingly light. The kids weren't all that happy about the prospect of moving to Israel, and the Cheerios were nonnegotiable.

Our new home was in the beach town of Hertzliya Pituach, only blocks from the Mediterranean Sea. The house had eight different levels, including two basements. Two separate rooftop decks offered views of the surrounding neighborhood, the newly constructed homes, and the rolling sand dunes that led to the ocean.

"Seven floors too many," was Orah's decided opinion, given that she had to spend her days running up and down the stairs, chasing Mikey from floor to floor while I worked in an air-conditioned high-rise, reviewing architectural plans. As someone who'd grown up sharing a room with two brothers and, at times, my parents, this house was a mansion. "Eight floors, countless rooms, but no telephone," Orah observed dryly. If we needed to make a call, we crossed the street to a retirement community and waited in line for the pay phone.

"True, but lots of Cheerios."

The American Commissary was fully stocked with all of the typical American foods we had grown accustomed to, which surprised and delighted us. It went a long way toward making Israel acceptable to our children at the beginning.

When I first saw Henri, I was taken aback. He was thinner than when I'd seen him just a couple of months earlier in June and there was an unfamiliar weariness in his voice. Stella was fretful and anxious, chain-smoking as a way to hide her worry. It was clear that Henri was very ill, and through the year that followed, he got thinner and weaker until the doctors told him it was time for him to leave the home he shared with Stella and check into a hospital.

He spent his last weeks under bright white hospital lights, hooked up to clear tubes, surrounded by beeping machines. Toward the end, he slept more and more until he seemed always to be sleeping. "Talk to him," the doctors said. Even though he seems like he's asleep, he may be listening."

And so we did. At first, feeling awkward and inhibited, I rambled, saying nothing real. Gradually I started to whisper the more important things, which are somehow often hardest to say: "I love you. I have always looked up to you." I told him things that would have made him smile. "You have an unparalleled gift for driving people crazy, and you were always the best at making Papa angry." It was a badge he wore with honor. My brother never met an authority figure he didn't want to challenge and, most of the time, he got away with it. He was, in fact, the only person I'd ever met who waged a battle against the Israeli Defense Forces (IDF) and won.

While Severin and I had served our compulsory military service without incident, Henri's military service was, perhaps unsurprisingly, marked by episodic bouts with authority, and he was frequently in trouble. One incident stood out. The IDF, recognizing Henri's artistic talent, assigned him to paint a large mural in the camp's mess hall. Henri started to work on the mural but he felt the need to take frequent breaks, and these breaks sometimes led to naps in the sun. When he was caught sleeping on duty, he ended up in the brig. Not one to be bothered by such constraints, he snuck out and went to the cinema, putting himself back in jail after the movie. This situation might have gone on indefinitely – snoozing in the brig, sneaking out when he wanted to attend the cinema – but his superior officers had a problem: Esteemed painter Marc Chagall was coming to visit the base, and the mural needed to be completed by the time he arrived.

Henri was released to resume work. "Ah, yes, but now the muse has left me, you see," he said as he strolled out of the jail. He spent many of the following days leaning back in a metal folding chair near the mural, legs stretched out, dozing in the sun and waiting for the muse to return. Finally, when Chagall was due to arrive in only days, and with a large blank spot still remaining in the center of the mural, Henri's muse instructed him to, rather hurriedly, paint a large white rectangle over the empty section. On top of that he painted red letters that read CENSORED. With the paint barely dry, Henri stood proudly next to his mural as Chagall, with his bird's nest hair and shy smile, walked by and complimented him on his work.

My irrepressible brother. He was a man who put his own unique stamp on the world. I could have told the IDF if only they'd asked me. I'd watched for years as my father tried to get Henri to bend to his will. If Father hadn't succeeded, the IDF didn't stand a chance.

Henri died of gastric cancer on September 12, 1980, three days after his 54th birthday. When we realized the end was close, we took shifts sitting with him, making sure he was never alone. I was holding his hand when he passed, free at last from the pain gnawing away at him.

At the conclusion of the air base project in 1982, our family returned to California. I reluctantly acknowledged that we were ill-suited for life in Israel. But Orah and I were the problem, not our children. They had adapted quickly, learning Hebrew, making friends, and excelling at school. They spent afternoons scrambling on sand dunes, swimming in the ocean, and mastering Space Invaders in the arcade at the Palace Hotel. But even though we'd both lived in Israel before, Orah and I were slower to reacclimate to the lack of infrastructure and the absence of luxuries we had come to take for granted. America had made us soft. We returned to Palo Alto, to our backyard barbecues and block parties, and to our large group of Israeli friends eager to welcome us back. Transplants like us, they cooked Israeli meals in modern kitchens and lived in homes with phones.

We went back to Israel every year or two. Since phone calls were expensive, we kept in touch mostly through letters in the intervening years. When I visited in the summer of 1989, several months after my mother had fallen and broken a hip, Severin warned me as we walked through the automatic doors of the retirement home to brace myself for what she would look like. "Mama's very frail. She never really recovered from her fall," he said. "She'll bruise if you look at her too hard."

I found my mother sunken into a wing chair, a crocheted blanket on her lap. She seemed smaller, with bird bones and parchment skin, but still very much my mother. Her mind and smile were intact, but I sensed she was receding into herself, drifting away from us as if being taken out to sea. I kissed her forehead as I left, overcome with the certainty it was the last time I would see her.

"I'll be back next year Mama, and I'll see you then," I lied, uselessly. We both knew.

In the parking lot, Severin and I sat in the car, heavy with the knowledge that soon it would be only the two of us. The windows were rolled down and I stared at the evergreen-shaped air freshener that dangled from the sedan's rearview mirror, turning in the breeze, oozing an artificial pine scent that was too sweet and lavatorial, nothing like a real tree. I sobbed quietly, tears streaming down my cheeks, overwhelmed by a deep feeling of loss. I was the one driving away, leaving to head back to California, but my mother was drifting out on the tide, a buoy at the horizon, about to vanish from view.

36

2016 TO NOW – HOMECOMING

I return to my courtyard in Paris every couple of years, drawn by the power of nostalgia, the memories of my time there and the people I knew, even though our neighbors are long gone. The Raymonds retired after we moved to Israel. Their son René stayed in the courtyard for a number of years after, selling his delicate music boxes out of an atelier, but one day when I knocked on the door and peeked my head into his shop, I was greeted by a young woman surrounded by sewing machines. René had moved, but I don't know where. Nor do I know what happened to Madame Nicolas or Monsieur Thibou. Once we left Paris, our family lost touch with them. But I think of them often, fondly, and with a deep sense of gratitude.

In July 2016 Orah and I visited Paris with our daughter, Karen, and her partner, Alexa. On that visit, through sheer coincidence, we were in Paris for le 14 Juillet, Bastille Day. That night we watched the fireworks explode over the Eiffel Tower, joining the crowd pressed together on the Pont de la Concorde, a bridge built out of stone pulled from the ruins of the Bastille prison. I couldn't help but think back to that night in 1937 when I watched them with my family, sitting on my father's shoulders at the World's Fair, unaware that my world was about to change forever. Sometimes it feels as if we are at a similar tipping point now.

After the fireworks we merged into the crowds at the Place de la Concorde, navigating through the swarm back towards our hotel near the Bastille. As we walked, our phones dinged with an alert: A truck had crashed into a mass of celebrators in Nice, an act of terrorism. Unknown numbers were dead and injured. The previous year had seen the terrorist attacks on

Charlie Hebdo and the Bataclan and several other venues. Now the crowds around us felt claustrophobic and we became hypervigilant, regarding a nearby white truck with suspicion, alert to the possibility that a similar event could happen here. These days, wars are fought differently.

The next day, July 15, is exactly 74 years to the day that Madame Nicolas knocked frantically on our apartment door to warn us of the coming arrest, to beg us to leave. I am planning to give Karen and Alexa a tour of my courtyard, to point up at the windows of my old apartment and the warehouse where we hid. I am not expecting to reenter the apartment, which I haven't been in since we moved to Israel in 1949. Or to reenter the flat where we hid for two years. But against all odds, that's what happens.

As we walk under the familiar stone tunnel that connects rue de Charonne to the courtyard interior, I immediately notice how clean everything is. Every time I return to my courtyard it seems freshly bathed; the building's walls are the color of buttermilk, rich and creamy, something a cat would lap up. There is none of the soot that previously glazed the courtyard, giving it a sort of industrial patina. Unlike the rest of us, the courtyard seems to be aging backwards. The 11th arrondissement is still known for woodworking and furniture, but most of the ateliers here are filled with white-collar professionals, people who design and consult rather than build. Thirteen stairways still run counterclockwise around the interior but the open entryways have been replaced by locked doors, protecting access. There's no doubt that the courtyard is prettier and more polished now, but part of me misses the way it used to look; the working-class vibrancy and the scruffy charm is gone.

There was a light rain this morning and when we arrive the cobblestones are shiny, as though they've been lacquered. It's quiet, almost startlingly so. I find the new concierge, a wiry man in a plaid cap; he lives in the same apartment the Raymonds used to occupy. I explain my history with the courtyard and he's eager to help, immediately ringing up the current owner of the apartment, who offers to let us in. It's an unexpected kindness. I've been back here countless times, but the closest I've been to the old apartment is the locked front door. Now it opens for me. I am excited and also – nervous? Yes, perhaps. I am approaching an old familiar, and I don't know how it will have changed. I think of Severin back in Israel. It's morning there as well and I picture him sitting in his favorite chair, a cup of tea in his hand. I wish he were here with me.

My head is noisy with racing thoughts and memories as we enter, but our group is quiet. The silence feels reverent, the way you remain quiet when you approach something sacred, even if it's just a memory. We step into the small apartment and I can see my family looking around and studying the space as if it's a museum, or an archeological artifact. We maneuver around each other carefully in the small flat, like people navigating a crowded exhibit.

The owner, Patrick, shows us around; the apartment is unoccupied, he uses it as an informal guest unit, a place for visiting friends to stay. It's different now, of course it is, but the changes are superficial and I can feel the bones of my old home underneath the smooth walls and modern decor. *Ah, yes, there you are my old friend.* The plywood dividing wall that my father built has been finished with drywall and is freshly painted, creating a true one-bedroom apartment. There is a small bathroom with shower, and a kitchenette. Our wood stove has been replaced by a round dining table. In the bedroom, between the windows where Henri's drafting table once lived, there is a computer on a small desk. Filled with Ikea furniture, it's the sort of urban apartment that might belong to a young, single professional. Given how gingerly the five of us walk around now, trying not to bump into anything or anyone, it's hard to believe that my family of five could have lived here happily all those years ago. But we did.

I can sense my family warming up. They have been whispering to each other, leaving me alone with my memories, but soon they are pointing, asking me questions. Alexa peers into the bathroom. *Wait,* she says. *You didn't have a bathroom, right, so what was here?* I explain that twin trundle beds previously occupied the space where the bathroom is and my brothers slept there. I point at a cabinet on the opposite wall. *My bed was there,* I say, *folded up during the day and opened each night.* I point to where I'm standing. *This is where our dining table was.* Karen turns around carefully. *Wow, Aba. Five of you lived here.* I'm not surprised at her amazement. She is also one of a family of five, and she grew up in a four-bedroom home that sometimes felt too small.

I walk into the bedroom and sit down on the bed. I'm facing rue de Charonne and the casement windows that look over it. The afternoon light filters through gauzy white curtains and it's the same light that I remember from all those years ago. Sitting here on this bed, looking at the unchanged view out of the windows, it's not hard for me to transport myself back in time and I feel myself getting choked up. Orah sits down next to me silently and takes my hand. She is not given to sentimentality – it's one of the things I love about her – but she knows how much it means for me to be back here. It's been 67 years. Tears roll silently down my cheeks as I think about all the life and love that these walls contained.

Patrick hands me a key to the apartment and says I'm welcome to use it any time. *Please stay here if you want. It's your apartment too.* I looked down at the key in my palm, moved by his gesture, and feel the emotion swell again. There's something special about this courtyard, and the people who live here.

The concierge has also arranged for us to visit the unit my family hid in for two years, at Stairway 6. It's been converted into an apartment – the warehouse merged with what used to be M. Thibou's workshop. An older couple, Lebanese immigrants, open the door and greet me in broken, halting French. The husband shows us around, grinning, a thin ring of white hair encircling his nut-brown head, while his wife, plump and smiley, makes tea. She is shy to talk. I speak to them in a simple, pidgin French that reminds me of the way Monsieur Roger spoke to my parents.

The changes in this unit are more dramatic and it's hard for me to imagine the old walls, to see where our wardrobe would have been, our mattresses, the wood stove in the corner. The windows are the same and I look out, remembering the countless hours I spent staring through the cloudy, dirt covered glass, longing to be outside. The Lebanese couple is happy to have visitors, and they want to talk about when I lived here, what it was like. I explain that I was just a boy, that it was many years ago. I don't tell them that I was in hiding during the Holocaust. I don't tell them that I am Jewish. Even now, in 2016, I am alert to the possibility that antisemitism might lurk beneath even the friendliest, kindest of faces.

I come back into the courtyard, into *my* courtyard, and look around again. The large patio is cleared of cars, sawdust and horse manure: No one works outside any longer. There are no singing Italians, no busking accordion players. Occasionally a well-dressed professional passes through, shoes clicking on the cobblestones, and disappears into one of the buildings. It's so quiet that any sound echoes off the courtyard walls and I'm once again startled by the change since I lived here. These buildings saw so much before I was born, and I suppose they will see even more after I am gone.

I've been told that the buildings at 5 rue de Charonne were originally a convent, one of the many that surrounded the nearby Saint-Antoine-des-Champs abbey. According to this history, there were once underground tunnels that led from 5 rue de Charonne directly into the belly of the Bastille; the nuns, clad in their long black and white habits, filed into the dark, narrow tunnels with tallow candles and crept along the dirt-floor route to the prison in order to care for the inmates. During my childhood a bell hung on the courtyard wall, far too high for even a tall adult to reach. But there had once been a long rope dangling from the bell, so that it could be rung to call the nuns to supper. The rope vanished before my time, and now even the bell is gone. At another point in its history, either before or after its time as a convent, 5 rue de Charonne apparently also housed French soldiers, the small apartments serving as barracks. Military horses stomped in the courtyard, their bridles secured to iron rings mounted by each stairway. There is only one ring remaining - by the entry to my old apartment, Stairway 1.

The word *cour*, French for courtyard, comes from the old French word *cort*, and further back the Latin word *cortem* [enclosed yard]. The French word for heart, *coeur*, is similar and has Latin roots as well, from *cor*. Those two French words, separated only by an "e," have very different pronunciations and origins. Yet I like to think of them as related, if not by blood then kinship. For a courtyard is, by design, at the center, or heart, of the buildings that surround it. More meaningfully, a courtyard is often the figurative heart of a place: the scene of casual banter, petty squabbles, deep and abiding friendships, tears of sorrow and joy. Our courtyard pumped life to the small ateliers that surrounded it, bringing work, commerce, and trade. But it also protected and sustained the lives of those who dwelled there.

When I think of the countless things that had to go right for us to survive the war, it feels like a miracle. One wrong turn, one different choice, and everything would have changed.

What if my parents had not immigrated to Paris, choosing instead to stay near family in Warsaw? We would have been imprisoned within the barbed wire of the Warsaw Ghetto in November 1940. Those of us who managed to survive the starvation and disease that ravaged the ghetto would have eventually been deported to one of the Polish camps. Every one of our relatives who remained in Poland perished, and we would have as well.

If Severin had answered honestly, "Yes, I am Issahar," when the gendarmes knocked on our apartment door in August 1941, he would have been sent to Drancy with my father.

If they had both been interned at Drancy, my father wouldn't have left the camp without Severin, even when released that November. Even deathly ill, he would not have left Severin behind.

If SS Capt. Dannecker hadn't left Drancy for those two pivotal days in November 1941, allowing the onsite doctors the chance to quietly release the internees who were most ill, my father would not have been one of 800 men – out of the approximately 70,000 people who came through Drancy – allowed to return home.

If on July 15, 1942, Madame Nicolas had not been at work.

Or if sitting at her desk at the Préfecture de Police, she had missed our typed names.

If she had seen the names but been afraid to leave work. Or unable to slip away. Without her warning, we would have been home when the gendarmes pounded on our door. So much came down to her decision to come home in the middle of the day to warn us. A woman who we knew only from passing her on the stairway.

If Monsieur and Madame Raymond had not acted as sentries, on the alert for any signs of trouble.

If Monsieur Thibou had shaken his head regretfully when my father asked him to harbor us. Where else could we have gone? Monsieur Thibou risked his own life *every day* to protect ours. For two years. He had nothing to gain, and so much to lose.

If Father, Severin, and Henri had not been able to work while we hid from the world, we would not have had francs to buy food.

If our shop-owner neighbors had not conspired as a group to set aside food for us, to have it waiting in brown paper packages for me. Without them, we would have starved.

If someone had heard my father when he raged in the middle of that terrible night, in the throes of his panic attack, and called the police, we would have been arrested. Once arrested, we would have been sent to Drancy, and then to Auschwitz.

If I had been discovered during my daily food run, by the miliciens or by any inquisitive gendarmes, I would have not known how to protect my family. A stern look and I would have folded, for I was just a child.

If, in the early days of our hiding, the looter, or whoever he was, who came to our door decided to report us.

If the milicien had not been convinced to stay quiet.

If the tradesman who whispered to Monsieur Raymond had simply gone directly to the police.

If any of the hundreds of workers who filed in and out of the courtyard each day, many of whom knew about us, had decided they wanted the reward that came with betraying us.

Or if they had believed the antisemitic propaganda and had decided that Jews were to blame for the problems of the world. That *we* were to blame.

Thankfully, none of those things happened. Instead, the unique alchemy of this particular courtyard – the coal-streaked, peeling walls that insulated us from the rest of Paris, the small community of people who lived here, the larger group of tradesmen who worked here – it all combined into something distinctive and enchanted, something that protected my family when we most needed it. This courtyard took care of its own. Madame

Nicolas warned us. Monsieur Thibou harbored us. The Reginauds, Meyers, Benots fed us. And the Raymonds protected us.

I wish I could thank those brave, wonderful people. I was a young boy then, but I am an old man now and I understand, in the way no child can, the enormity of their risk. I feel immense gratitude when I think of them. The gratitude lives deep within me, as if in the marrow of my bones.

Righteous Among the Nations is an honorific used to describe non-Jews who risked their lives during the Holocaust to save Jewish people. Recipients of this recognition are awarded a medal and their names are added to the Wall of Honor, which is actually a series of stone walls nestled among the carob trees in the Garden of the Righteous in Jerusalem. If I could, I would have all our neighbors listed on the Wall of Honor. They were each crucial to keeping us safe and alive. At the very least, Monsieur Thibou and Madame Nicolas, who risked the most, should be counted as righteous. Their names should be inscribed on the wall. These kind, brave people weren't family. They weren't even friends, not by most people's definition. We had little in common. We didn't share a religion or heritage. In the case of my parents, we barely spoke the same language. Taught to be respectful of adults, I never even knew their first names. We never had a meal together, and we didn't visit each other's homes. They were our neighbors. And, for them, that was enough.

They should be Righteous Among the Nations, yet it's a debt I cannot repay because I don't have enough information about them to nominate them. Because I owe them something, I have written down this story. In place of medals and names etched into a wall, I have typed out these words. It is not nearly enough, but it will have to suffice, at least for now. Maybe someday my words will be read by someone who knew them, who recognizes in my description a grandparent or a family friend. If not, then at least you who have read this far will know the truth. In a working-class courtyard in Paris, during the darkest period of World War II, a small group of people came together to save a Jewish family. Compared to the story of many Jews during the Holocaust, not that much happened. And because not much happened, everything has been possible.

Me (right) and Henri (left) sitting at the window of the apartment at 5 rue de Charonne in 1946.

Me, sitting in the window of my family's Paris apartment in July of 2016.

The courtyard over the years. View from the middle of courtyard, looking toward the entry tunnel at rue de Charonne.

View into courtyard interior from my old
apartment window, July 2016.

The Parket family gathered in 2016. From left to right: Mike with wife Rosie, who is holding
grandson Max. Grandchildren Mikaela, Dylan and Tegan. Ben is in the center, with grandson Cooper.
Orah Parket, with grandson Aiden. David, Karen, David's partner Brian and Karen's partner Alexa.

ACKNOWLEDGMENTS

I am deeply grateful to my family for their unwavering patience and support throughout this long writing process — one that took far longer than any of us had anticipated. Thank you for reading the early drafts of the book and providing invaluable feedback. A special shout-out to my wife, Karen (Ben's daughter), whose constant support and enthusiasm were a steady source of strength. She read countless versions of the manuscript with genuine interest and dedication. I am also incredibly thankful to my mom, Susan, whose sharp eye and tireless efforts as a proofreader were indispensable. My thanks also go to Rachel M., who generously read and offered insightful feedback on an early version of the book. I truly don't know what I would have done without my editor, Beth Rashbaum, whose encouragement kept me going and whose expert guidance transformed this book into something far greater than I could have imagined. My heartfelt thanks also go to Liesbeth Heenk for founding Amsterdam Publishers and dedicating her life to giving Holocaust survivors a platform to share their stories. Finally, I owe a huge debt of gratitude to Ben himself, who entrusted me with his story and whose life continues to inspire me.

ABOUT THE AUTHORS

Ben Parket was born in Paris in 1933 to parents that emigrated from Poland. In 1942, targeted by Nazis and the French collaborators, he and his family went into hiding in their courtyard. Ben is a retired architect, the father of three children, grandfather to six, who recently celebrated his 91st birthday. He lived in Paris and Tel Aviv before settling happily in Northern California 60 years ago. This is his first book.

Alexa Morris grew up in the suburbs of Washington DC, dabbling in a number of jobs (Senate page, vet tech, retail) before choosing the world of non-profits, where she remains to this day. She is married to Ben's daughter and they live in Northern California. In her spare time, she loves hiking and throwing wonky ceramics on the wheel. She is currently at work on her first novel.

AMSTERDAM PUBLISHERS
HOLOCAUST LIBRARY

The series **Holocaust Survivor Memoirs World War II** consists of the following autobiographies of survivors:

Outcry. Holocaust Memoirs, by Manny Steinberg

Hank Brodt Holocaust Memoirs. A Candle and a Promise, by Deborah Donnelly

The Dead Years. Holocaust Memoirs, by Joseph Schupack

Rescued from the Ashes. The Diary of Leokadia Schmidt, Survivor of the Warsaw Ghetto, by Leokadia Schmidt

My Lvov. Holocaust Memoir of a twelve-year-old Girl, by Janina Hescheles

Remembering Ravensbrück. From Holocaust to Healing, by Natalie Hess

Wolf. A Story of Hate, by Zeev Scheinwald with Ella Scheinwald

Save my Children. An Astonishing Tale of Survival and its Unlikely Hero, by Leon Kleiner with Edwin Stepp

Holocaust Memoirs of a Bergen-Belsen Survivor & Classmate of Anne Frank, by Nanette Blitz Konig

Defiant German - Defiant Jew. A Holocaust Memoir from inside the Third Reich, by Walter Leopold with Les Leopold

In a Land of Forest and Darkness. The Holocaust Story of two Jewish Partisans, by Sara Lustigman Omelinski

Holocaust Memories. Annihilation and Survival in Slovakia, by Paul Davidovits

From Auschwitz with Love. The Inspiring Memoir of Two Sisters' Survival, Devotion and Triumph Told by Manci Grunberger Beran & Ruth Grunberger Mermelstein, by Daniel Seymour

Remetz. Resistance Fighter and Survivor of the Warsaw Ghetto, by Jan Yohay Remetz

My March Through Hell. A Young Girl's Terrifying Journey to Survival, by Halina Kleiner with Edwin Stepp

Roman's Journey, by Roman Halter

Beyond Borders. Escaping the Holocaust and Fighting the Nazis. 1938-1948, by Rudi Haymann

The Engineers. A memoir of survival through World War II in Poland and Hungary, by Henry Reiss

Spark of Hope. An Autobiography, by Luba Wrobel Goldberg

Footnote to History. From Hungary to America. The Memoir of a Holocaust Survivor, by Andrew Laszlo

Farewell Atlantis. Recollections, by Valentīna Freimane

The Mulberry Tree. The story of a life before and after the Holocaust, by Iboja Wandall-Holm

The Boy in the Back. A True Story of Survival in Auschwitz and Mauthausen, by Fern Lebo

The Courtyard. A memoir, by Benjamin Parket and Alexa Morris

Beneath the Lightless Sky. Surviving the Holocaust in the Sewers of Lvov, by Ignacy Chiger

Run, Mendel Run, by Milton H. Schwartz

The series **Holocaust Survivor True Stories** consists of the following biographies:

Among the Reeds. The true story of how a family survived the Holocaust,
by Tammy Bottner

A Holocaust Memoir of Love & Resilience. Mama's Survival from Lithuania to
America, by Ettie Zilber

Living among the Dead. My Grandmother's Holocaust Survival Story of Love and
Strength, by Adena Bernstein Astrowsky

Heart Songs. A Holocaust Memoir, by Barbara Gilford

Shoes of the Shoah. The Tomorrow of Yesterday, by Dorothy Pierce

Hidden in Berlin. A Holocaust Memoir, by Evelyn Joseph Grossman

Separated Together. The Incredible True WWII Story of Soulmates Stranded an
Ocean Apart, by Kenneth P. Price, Ph.D.

The Man Across the River. The incredible story of one man's will to survive the
Holocaust, by Zvi Wiesenfeld

If Anyone Calls, Tell Them I Died. A Memoir, by Emanuel (Manu) Rosen

The House on Thrömerstrasse. A Story of Rebirth and Renewal in the Wake of the
Holocaust, by Ron Vincent

Dancing with my Father. His hidden past. Her quest for truth. How Nazi Vienna
shaped a family's identity, by Jo Sorochinsky

The Story Keeper. Weaving the Threads of Time and Memory - A Memoir,
by Fred Feldman

Krisia's Silence. The Girl who was not on Schindler's List, by Ronny Hein

Defying Death on the Danube. A Holocaust Survival Story,
by Debbie J. Callahan with Henry Stern

A Doorway to Heroism. A decorated German-Jewish Soldier who became an
American Hero, by W. Jack Romberg

The Shoemaker's Son. The Life of a Holocaust Resister, by Laura Beth Bakst

The Redhead of Auschwitz. A True Story, by Nechama Birnbaum

Land of Many Bridges. My Father's Story, by Bela Ruth Samuel Tenenholtz

Creating Beauty from the Abyss. The Amazing Story of Sam Herciger, Auschwitz Survivor and Artist, by Lesley Ann Richardson

On Sunny Days We Sang. A Holocaust Story of Survival and Resilience, by Jeannette Grunhaus de Gelman

Painful Joy. A Holocaust Family Memoir, by Max J. Friedman

I Give You My Heart. A True Story of Courage and Survival, by Wendy Holden

In the Time of Madmen, by Mark A. Prelas

Monsters and Miracles. Horror, Heroes and the Holocaust, by Ira Wesley Kitmacher

Flower of Vlora. Growing up Jewish in Communist Albania, by Anna Kohen

Aftermath: Coming of Age on Three Continents. A Memoir, by Annette Libeskind Berkovits

Not a real Enemy. The True Story of a Hungarian Jewish Man's Fight for Freedom, by Robert Wolf

Zaidy's War. Four Armies, Three Continents, Two Brothers. One Man's Impossible Story of Endurance, by Martin Bodek

The Glassmaker's Son. Looking for the World my Father left behind in Nazi Germany, by Peter Kupfer

The Apprentice of Buchenwald. The True Story of the Teenage Boy Who Sabotaged Hitler's War Machine, by Oren Schneider

Good for a Single Journey, by Helen Joyce

Burying the Ghosts. She escaped Nazi Germany only to have her life torn apart by the woman she saved from the camps: her mother, by Sonia Case

American Wolf. From Nazi Refugee to American Spy. A True Story, by Audrey Birnbaum

Bipolar Refugee. A Saga of Survival and Resilience, by Peter Wiesner

In the Wake of Madness. My Family's Escape from the Nazis, by Bettie Lennett Denny

Before the Beginning and After the End, by Hymie Anisman

I Will Give Them an Everlasting Name. Jacksonville's Stories of the Holocaust,
by Samuel Cox

Hiding in Holland. A Resistance Memoir, by Shulamit Reinharz

The Ghosts on the Wall. A Grandson's Memoir of the Holocaust, by Kenneth D. Wald

Thirteen in Auschwitz. My grandmother's fight to stay human,
by Lauren Meyerowitz Port

Dreaming of the River, by Pauline Steinhorn

The series **Jewish Children in the Holocaust** consists of the following autobiographies of Jewish children hidden during WWII in the Netherlands:

Searching for Home. The Impact of WWII on a Hidden Child, by Joseph Gosler

Sounds from Silence. Reflections of a Child Holocaust Survivor, Psychiatrist and Teacher, by Robert Krell

Sabine's Odyssey. A Hidden Child and her Dutch Rescuers, by Agnes Schipper

The Journey of a Hidden Child,

by Harry Pila and Robin Black

The series **New Jewish Fiction** consists of the following novels, written by Jewish authors. All novels are set in the time during or after the Holocaust.

The Corset Maker. A Novel, by Annette Libeskind Berkovits

Escaping the Whale. The Holocaust is over. But is it ever over for the next generation? by Ruth Rotkowitz

When the Music Stopped. Willy Rosen's Holocaust, by Casey Hayes

Hands of Gold. One Man's Quest to Find the Silver Lining in Misfortune, by Roni Robbins

The Girl Who Counted Numbers. A Novel, by Roslyn Bernstein

There was a garden in Nuremberg. A Novel, by Navina Michal Clemerson

The Butterfly and the Axe, by Omer Bartov

To Live Another Day. A Novel, by Elizabeth Rosenberg

The Right to Happiness. After all they went through. Stories, by Helen Schary Motro

Five Amber Beads,
by Richard Aronowitz

To Love Another Day. A Novel,
by Elizabeth Rosenberg

Cursing the Darkness. A Novel about Loss and Recovery, by Joanna Rosenthall

The series **Holocaust Heritage** consists of the following memoirs by 2G:

The Cello Still Sings. A Generational Story of the Holocaust and of the
Transformative Power of Music, by Janet Horvath

The Fire and the Bonfire. A Journey into Memory, by Ardyn Halter

The Silk Factory: Finding Threads of My Family's True Holocaust Story,
by Michael Hickins

Winter Light. The Memoir of a Child of Holocaust Survivors, by Grace Feuerverger

Out from the Shadows. Growing up with Holocaust Survivor Parents,
by Willie Handler

Hidden in Plain Sight. A Family Memoir and the Untold Story of the Holocaust in
Serbia, by Julie Brill

The Unspeakable. Breaking my family's silence surrounding the Holocaust,
by Nicola Hanefeld

Eighteen for Life. Surviving the Holocaust,

by Helen Schamroth

Austrian Again. Reclaiming a Lost Legacy,

by Anne Hand

The series **Holocaust Books for Young Adults** consists of the following novels, based on true stories:

The Boy behind the Door. How Salomon Kool Escaped the Nazis. Inspired by a True Story, by David Tabatsky

Running for Shelter. A True Story, by Suzette Sheft

The Precious Few. An Inspirational Saga of Courage based on True Stories, by David Twain with Art Twain

Dark Shadows Hover, by Jordan Steven Sher

The Sun will Shine Again, by Cynthia Goldstein Monsour

The series **WWII Historical Fiction** consists of the following novels, some of which are based on true stories:

Mendelevski's Box. A Heartwarming and Heartbreaking Jewish Survivor's Story, by Roger Swindells

A Quiet Genocide. The Untold Holocaust of Disabled Children in WWII Germany, by Glenn Bryant

The Knife-Edge Path, by Patrick T. Leahy

Brave Face. The Inspiring WWII Memoir of a Dutch/German Child, by I. Caroline Crocker and Meta A. Evenbly

When We Had Wings. The Gripping Story of an Orphan in Janusz Korczak's Orphanage. A Historical Novel, by Tami Shem-Tov

Jacob's Courage. Romance and Survival amidst the Horrors of War, by Charles S. Weinblatt

A Semblance of Justice. Based on true Holocaust experiences, by Wolf Holles

Under the Pink Triangle. Where forbidden love meets unspeakable evil, by Katie Moore

Amsterdam Publishers Newsletter

Subscribe to our Newsletter by selecting the menu at the top (right) of
amsterdampublishers.com

www.ingramcontent.com/pod-product-compliance
Lightning Source LLC
LaVergne TN
LVHW090737300425
809782LV00005B/15